the book of trouble

also by ann marlowe

how to stop time: heroin from a to z

the book of trouble

a romance

ann marlowe

harcourt, inc.

orlando   austin   new york
san diego   toronto   london

www.HarcourtBooks.com

Library of Congress Cataloging-in-Publication Data
Marlowe, Ann, 1958–
The book of trouble: a romance/Ann Marlowe.—1st ed.
p.   cm.
1. Marlowe, Ann, 1958–   2. Marlowe, Ann, 1958—Travel.
3. Man-woman relationships—United States.   4. Jewish women—
United States—Biography.   5. Afghanistan—Description and travel.
I. Title.
CT275.M199A3 2006
915.8104'47—dc22   2005002403
ISBN-13: 978-0151-01131-5   ISBN-10: 0-15-101131-1

Text set in Legacy Serif Book
Designed by Linda Lockowitz

Printed in the United States of America

First edition
K J I H G F E D C B A

contents

prologue | *i've memorized your body*   1

part one

1   *war crimes*   7
2   *a seventeen-year-old virgin*   13
3   *satan is the third*   19
4   *the morning of the world*   27
5   *i have a sheep*   37
6   *fifty years are not enough*   55
7   *we are nicer because we have no rules*   71

part two

8   *voulez-vous coucher avec moi ce soir?*   81
9   *a love letter*   93
10   *who are your ancestors?*   103
11   *delightful to date*   111
12   *a pashtun party dress*   115
13   *foreign hands, part one*   125
14   *deli rose*   135

15   *learning to make aash*   145

16   *ten years, part one*   153

17   *plenty of time*   159

18   *i am trying to get packed and ready to go*   171

19   *they have all ultimately behaved like cads*   181

part three

20   *be silent that the lord who gave you speech may talk*   197

21   *cousin marriages galore*   207

22   *ten years, part two*   219

23   *a bottle of good scotch*   227

24   *between the onion and its skin*   235

25   *people don't fall in love anymore*   241

26   *you can go around by the back door*   247

27   *fake arabic*   253

28   *foreign hands, part two*   261

glossary of farsi and arabic words   273

acknowledgments   275

author's note   279

the book of trouble

prologue | *i've memorized your body*

It's one on a Sunday afternoon, but the late February sun hasn't reached the skylight above my bed. Amir and I have been lying here since five in the morning, when we stopped making love on the living-room couch and climbed the three flights of stairs to my room. We haven't slept. Amir and I don't sleep when we're together, and we don't leave my house. When we talk, sleep deprivation pushes our bursts of speech toward free association; we never stay on a topic for long, except, sometimes, Afghanistan, which drew us together. When we get hungry we don't go out to eat or order in, in the way of people in Manhattan. We cook Afghan food that Amir remembers from his Herat childhood and I from two recent trips, or eggs, which he says are every Afghan's favorite breakfast.

Mostly what we do is make love, again and again, more than either of us has before, yet not enough to quench desire, or bring fatigue or pain. When Amir said *making love* on our first night four weeks ago, I'd almost made fun of him. I'd never spoken those words aloud before; I was used to talking about *having sex*. But as the night turns to day, his words seem the only way to describe what's happening between us. I've never known physical sensation to become emotion so immediately.

I've loved men I thought were better looking. When I look hard at him I have to admit Amir's not my type: no better than average in height, short armed, barrel-chested. Though he's tremendously strong, he doesn't have the toned muscles of American men who've played sports all their lives. Usually I like that sort: tall, with long-limbed, elegant bodies. But I can't let go of this one.

I've had lovers who were technically better in bed, more imaginative or skilled, or psychologically more knowing, intuiting exactly how my desire worked. There's no art in what Amir does with me, and I don't think he's had nearly as much experience as I have. How could he, he's ten years younger, thirty-four to my forty-four, and in his words, *conservative in bed.* He tries hard to pretend that the taboos of the culture and religion he takes seriously no longer influence his sexual life. But when he shyly asks if I've ever considered a threesome, he's taken aback when I answer too quickly that the few I've had were great. Taboos are still real to him, so sex is momentous for him in a way it never is with the Americans I go to bed with. And the flip side of his naïveté—Amir's obvious delight in my body, the way he puts sex first—is something I've been looking for all my life.

It's one thirty now: I kiss the spot I love on the back of Amir's neck and ask, Aren't you hungry, will you let me take you out to brunch? We've never eaten in a restaurant alone, and he always buys the groceries when we cook. He smiles and doesn't let go of me and says, So we can pretend to be normal people? This sort of joking is as close as we ever come to talking about what is going on between us. Our time together is shadowed by his leaving. By the Persian New Year a month from now, he'll be back in Afghanistan for the first time in twenty years, and he says he'll stay at least six months. Anything could happen then.

Whatever is happening between us might mean very little against the pull of custom. I know Amir's past: he fought the Russians as a teenager, and many of his relatives died in that war. He can bear any cruelty, so he can inflict any pain. He will feel remorse, but he can bear that, too. What I see in his eyes: sadness, intelligence, complete impenetrability sometimes, fondness other times, but no tenderness. I don't know if I can trust him with my heart, if I have any hold on him at all beyond his passion for my body.

He says he's evenly divided between two cultures, but he seems more Afghan to me. Amir won't kiss me on the lips or even hold me in front of other people, except his closest friends. When I kissed him in Central Park one afternoon, he bristled and mumbled, Public displays of affection. I asked, Does that make you uncomfortable?, and his *no* was without conviction.

There are consolations. He hates makeup on women and high heels leave him cold. When I ask what clothing excites him, he says, Something that comes off quickly. Alone in his apartment in Brooklyn, he confides, he wears *shalwar kameez,* Afghan traditional dress of tunic and baggy trousers. I would love to see him this way, but he hasn't invited me to his place.

I'm secretly disappointed that Amir wants to settle in New York. Three months after my last trip, I still miss Afghanistan with a sharpness that surprises me. Sometimes I imagine living in

Mazar-i-Sharif part of the year; I dream of blending the two cultures. But Amir may not feel the same. I fell in love with the rich, archaic humanity of Afghanistan. And underneath his preppy clothes I see hints of this in Amir: a stillness, a warmth, and a naïveté I want to protect. But maybe what attracts him to me are some American traits I want to change. He might admire my facade of cynicism, my way of putting intellect first. I worry with him, as I have before with other men, that I'm not good at saying how much he means to me. What has he heard of my feelings, really—a *honey* here or there. But he knows, I'm sure. I hope.

After a quarter century of dating, I'm tired of pretending that I don't care about a man so that he'll like me more, I'm tired of the relentless calculus of self-interest that so many women I know fall into when they talk about what used to be called love. I don't want to have a "relationship," much less a "committed relationship," a phrase that has always evoked mental hospitals to me. I want to meet someone and fall in love and live with him all the rest of my days.

The winter light finally creeps in at the edges of the blinds on the skylight. The clock is nearing two. We're both starved, we should go out to eat, but we can't seem to let go of each other.

Clinging to Amir, I'm terrified when I blurt out, I've memorized your body. And I'm surprised when he says, The same is true for me—so surprised I don't weep as I'm afraid I might. For just a moment, I can't believe my luck. How often does this happen in a lifetime?

I have no idea at all that this will be the second-to-last day I spend in bed with Amir.

part one

I hope I meet you in the afterlife,
because fifty years together was not enough.

—Uzbek folk saying, aged husband to wife,
northern Afghanistan

I'd gone out of my way to avoid thinking of Amir sexually from the moment I met him, eight months before, in early June of 2002.

It was at a party, and I was reeling from my reentry to American life after my first trip to Afghanistan. Normally I love parties, but that night I found the effort to make small talk exhausting. I told the host that I was leaving, although it was barely midnight.

"Wait, you should meet Amir; he's from Afghanistan. Meet Ann, she just got back from Mazar-i-Sharif last week."

A powerfully built man with thick black hair, a hooked nose, and skin the same olive tone as mine was leaning against the kitchen counter that doubled as the bar. He looked to be in his late thirties, maybe older. His clothes couldn't have been more ordinary, a blue striped Brooks Brothers shirt and blue blazer over chinos. There was something a little rumpled about him that reminded me of the prep school boys at Harvard who wore the same white shirt and blazer they'd had to wear in boarding school, but with a defiant *déshabillé*. You were to know they'd gone to an elite school but had become too cool for all that. That effect would have been completed with a battered pair of Top-Siders. But this man had light tan loafers of cheap-looking leather. Immigrant shoes, living-in-Queens shoes.

Amir's slouch, though, was challenging, even arrogant, in a familiar American way. It was nothing like the body language of the men I'd met in Afghanistan a couple of weeks before. They had confounded my expectations of stereotypical mountain warriors, proverbial "fierce Afghans"; they were quieter and gentler than Americans, their voices softer, their way of holding themselves dignified but never aggressive.

From the start, I responded to Amir differently than I would have to a Western man. I'd taken the warnings of my friends with more experience in Afghanistan to heart: no body language that could be construed as flirtation, and never offer more physical contact than shaking a man's hand on greeting and leave-taking.

So I said hello to Amir stiffly in Dari: *Sh'ma khub asteed?*

Amir broke into a smile. Lots of Americans had been going to Afghanistan lately—it was all too fashionable—but few bothered to learn Afghan Persian, or Dari.

Judging my abilities correctly—I'd only been studying for a month—he answered in English, I'm fine, how are you?

There might have been a note of mild parody in his reply. I laughed, and he continued, What were you doing in Mazar?

A friend of mine is friends with General Dostum from the early nineties. After the Taliban fell, he wanted to go back, and he took me and another American woman with him.

Dostum is a controversial figure, the unelected ruler of a good chunk of northern Afghanistan. American newspapers call him a warlord, but his forces were key in defeating the Taliban; and he supports women's education and voting rights.

Amir's warm brown eyes narrowed. He should be tried as a war criminal, he said.

I remembered my dinners at Dostum's table and how his obsidian eyes had gradually opened as he grew comfortable with my presence one night. I watched as an Afghan woman argued fiercely with him and was amazed at his patience. I would never have been the guest of a politician I thought was a war criminal, though I knew that Dostum, like the late Ahmed Shah Massoud, bore some responsibility for the destruction of Kabul in the early nineties.

That's ridiculous. No politician's hands in Afghanistan are clean, but...

And I argued with Amir. Soon I heard myself getting too heated. Afghanistan was not my country, and it was Amir's. I am known for not backing down from a disagreement, but this time I decided to avoid a full-on confrontation. I told Amir I had to leave.

And then I did something else I rarely did with a man. I asked for Amir's card. I did it because I wasn't attracted to him, because my interest was purely in the Afghan connection, or so I would have said. Anything or anyone having to do with Afghanistan was fascinating to me in the full flush of my infatuation with the country.

I read the name of the consulting firm on the card. I know your firm! I worked at your main competition twenty years ago. (What a hell job that had been.) Do you like it?

I'm an engineer. (Maybe that explained the shoes.) They have me doing pretty specialized assignments. It's fine, I don't have to travel that much. Are you still in consulting?

I'm a writer. I've published a book, and I write book reviews, pieces on politics. I did a *New York Post* op-ed about my trip. But I make my living in business. I'm a headhunter for tax and pension lawyers—it's an odd little niche. Listen, I'd like to talk more, but I'm still jet-lagged. It was nice to meet you, Amir.

The next day, I carefully entered Amir's information in my computer so I could get in touch with him before my next trip to Afghanistan. I didn't like his politics, but even so I had fun talking with him. Maybe it was that I've never met an Afghan who spoke such good English or seemed so westernized. Even the returned Afghan American exiles I'd met in Afghanistan had more rough edges—endearing rough edges to be sure, but qualities in their speech and dress and manner that made me think they'd be out of place in my social life. No matter how aristocratic their families were in Afghanistan, in America they registered as immigranty.

Four months later, in October, I arranged to go back to Afghanistan for four weekes. This time I was going to teach English at the university and buy supplies for some of the pitiful primary schools I visited the first time around. I also wanted to broaden my exposure beyond Dostum's circle and region. So I e-mailed Amir and invited him to talk about Afghanistan over coffee; I promised not to become too vehement. His response was eager and friendly—maybe he'd forgotten our spat. Something made me suggest that he come to my house for a coffee, but I picked a day when my housekeeper would be there. From my experience in Afghanistan, I figured that Amir might be uncomfortable being alone with a woman, or assume that I meant to seduce him. I dressed conservatively and didn't offer him alcohol.

Sitting on my living-room couch and sipping the water he'd asked for, Amir told me about himself. His family were well-connected Pashtun landowners from the mixed Pashtun and Tajik area near Herat. That made Amir the first Pashtun I'd met; the region I'd visited around Mazar was largely Uzbek. In the news coverage of the war against the Taliban I was taken with the beauty of the bearded Pashtun tribesmen, but I also absorbed some of the liberal American prejudice against this ethnic group, who'd provided the power base for the Taliban. They had a reputation as socially conservative, headstrong, and warlike. They were towelheads who toted guns and oppressed their women. Yet Amir had gone to Princeton, I learned, and seemed the soul of reason.

Anger crept into his voice only when he talked about how he'd been trying to return to Afghanistan ever since the fall of the Taliban.

I keep waiting and waiting for my green card. I'd like to go for a long trip. Maybe I'll work for the government. They can use American-trained engineers. I haven't been back since we fled to Pakistan in 1982, when I was fourteen.

So you're thirty-four? I tried to keep the surprise from my voice. He looked years older, and I liked that. He had some character to his face. At my age I was unable to see anything but generic youth in many thirty-four-year-old faces.

Yeah, I'm old to be an associate. I went to grad school for a year in Houston, then I started a company with one of my cousins there, but it didn't go very well. Dot-com. I thought I was going to be a millionaire, but we got caught in the dot-com bust. After that, I took the first good job I was offered in New York and moved to Brooklyn. I was lucky to get hired before 9/11.

I looked at the clock and realized I had to leave for a friend's reading. Somehow an hour and a half had gone by, and we'd never even talked politics. We'd have to do something about that. But when Amir returned a few days later (this time without the housekeeper present), we never got to politics. In fact, after he left I couldn't remember much of what we talked about at all—only a sense of pleasure.

2 | a seventeen-year-old virgin

"The Western idea of romantic love is an illusion. I don't believe in it. I want to have an arranged marriage." Amir glances around my long dinner table to see how we're taking this. His deep brown eyes are calm, his broad face relaxed. My other guests look up from their salmon steaks and risotto with fall vegetables, waiting for the punch line or the explanation.

Amir smiles coyly, and for the first time in our brief friendship, I wonder about his love life. In the few weeks since I first invited him to my house, I've described him to my women friends as handsome, and I enjoy his physical presence at my table, but I've never thought about him as a sexual being before. When we talked alone, he never mentioned his marital status, much less his feelings about marriage.

Amir continues. "I want to marry an Afghan girl. A seventeen-year-old virgin." He lingers over the first syllable of *virgin,* stroking it.

And then all hell breaks loose.

"Well, if American men could get seventeen-year-old virgins that way, they'd be having arranged marriages, too." Shirin, my Persian tutor, smiles, amused. She's Amir's age, thirty-four, though she looks about twenty. I wonder if she and Amir might make a good couple. I met her just two days after I met Amir, in early June, and over four months of twice-weekly lessons, I've grown to know her much better than I know Amir, but I don't know if she will like him or not. The Afghan-Iranian combination could be tricky. Like most upper-class Iranians, Shirin views Afghans with a benevolent condescension. They're the provincial branch of the family who kept ancient Persian culture and speech alive, but they're also backwards and take religion too seriously. (In return, Afghans consider Iranians effeminate and overly influenced by European culture.)

"You think women are either virgins or whores? Did they teach you that at Princeton?" Luisa likes controversy, but this time her sharp words don't seem calculated. Her voice is strained, and I see from the way she tosses her golden blond hair that she's genuinely outraged. She's seen the cult of feminine purity at work in South America, the ruling-class men she grew up with who go to brothels while expecting to marry virgins. It's part of why she's chosen to live in New York, despite the advantages she'd have in Caracas from her family's name and social position. And I think these feelings of outrage are part of why she's unmarried at forty, after twenty years of being a celebrated beauty.

"Why would you want a seventeen-year-old? You're what, almost forty, aren't you?" Jason shakes his head in disapproval, his rich Etonian voice melodious even in criticism, and he glances at Luisa. I've invited them here to meet each other, and so far my strategy is working. He's a writer like Luisa, and successful enough to not be intimidated by her intensity.

My friends are angry at Amir, angrier than I am. I have the American luxury of being amused at Amir's tribal customs. Everyone else around the table was born overseas: Iran, Turkey, Greece, Venezuela, England. Everyone except Jason came to New York in part to escape practices like marrying a virgin or staying one. It rarely occurs to me to wonder why most of my close friends are foreign-born. I assume it's something along the lines of sharing a sense of distance. But tonight it occurs to me that the foreign countries my friends are from aren't the other advanced democracies. They're places just emerging from the Third World, places that aren't quite modern.

Amir tries to explain that an arranged marriage to a virgin is Afghan tradition, but he can hardly get a word in edgewise, and he doesn't raise his voice. I'm not sure if he's upset about the ruckus he's caused or basking in the attention. When the talk turns to the Afghan practice of paying a bride-price for a woman, he defends this, too.

I object, "But it's so close to prostitution, don't you see? Buying and selling women doesn't give them much dignity." I begin an argument: "What would you do if your sister told you she'd decided to become a prostitute?"

Amir tenses immediately, although I know by now that he has only brothers. "I'd ki—" Then he catches himself in time and begins again. "I'd tell her . . ."

Everyone talks at once, and over the din I hear Luisa's voice: "I heard what you wanted to say!" For her, Amir's desire to kill his nonexistent sister is the stuff of tragedy, not comedy. I hope her fervor won't scare Jason off.

Amir excuses himself to go upstairs to the bathroom, and I can't tell if he's shaken. His dark brown eyes give little away. Even if he's enjoying the attention, I feel bad that he's come under attack in my house. In Afghanistan I was treated with grace even when I expressed opinions contrary to my hosts'. Amir deserves no less in my house. But my guests gossip about Amir in his absence. When Jason says in his dulcet tones, "He may have gone to Princeton, but he's still a savage," I know that's part of what I like about Amir. And then I wonder how calculated this savage aspect might be on Amir's part.

When Amir returns to the table, I try to smooth things over, insisting to the other guests that there are good things about traditional Afghan society that Westerners can learn from. The outrage peters out eventually, and because it's a work night, the dinner draws to a close along with the controversy. Just as the party is breaking up, Amir mentions his friend Luca.

"Luca di Pizzicatti?" Jason asks. "I know him."

"So do I," Luisa says slowly, cocking her head at Amir. "The best-looking cokehead in Milano in the nineties. A friend of mine dated him for a while."

"I know Luca from Princeton," Amir says primly. "We played

on the squash team together, but he was a senior when I was a sophomore. If he was doing drugs then, I didn't know about it."

Luisa lets it drop, but later, when it's just her and Jason and me, she says, "That proves it—if he's friends with Luca, Amir is pretty Americanized. Pretty decadent. I know that whole crowd. Believe you me, Amir doesn't really care about marrying a virgin, he just knows how to work it. He knows that American women eat up his savage Afghan act. Guess what he said to me when you were clearing away the dishes? 'A wife is for the kitchen. That's how I was brought up.'"

She pauses and looks at me. "You're not interested in him, are you?"

I raise my eyebrows, as though this were the dumbest question in the world.

3 | *satan is the third*

After the dinner, I only have two weeks in New York before leaving for Afghanistan. They pass in a blur of happiness that I attribute to the trip. I see Amir several times, more than I see any of my other friends, but it doesn't occur to me that this means anything because we're always with Shirin. I've been encouraging a romance, inviting them together, and they seem to get on well, although she says, "I don't date men who look like that. I like tall, thin ones." But I'm confident in my match-making abilities: Luisa and Jason have been dating since they met at my dinner.

One night Amir and Shirin and I have been hanging out for a few hours in my house, and we're getting hungry. I don't want to disrupt our rapport by moving to a restaurant, so I tell them I'll go around the corner to my favorite Indian place and bring back some tandoori chicken.

"Are you sure you want to take the risk of leaving us alone?" Amir asks, his eyes glinting. "The Prophet Mohammed says that when a man and a woman are alone together, the third party is Satan."

Shirin smiles indulgently, though she's not at all religious, and I'm convinced my plan is working. The glint in Amir's eyes is surely for her, although his remark makes me wonder about the evenings he was alone with me in my house before the dinner party. Each time I've seen him, I've worn clothes that don't show my figure. I want to avoid giving Amir the idea that I'm attracted to him. I don't want to make a fool of myself. I'm ten years older than he is, and he wants to marry a seventeen-year-old. Shirin isn't seventeen, but at least she's his age and speaks his language. (Iranian and Afghan Farsi are related approximately as American and Scottish English. The Afghan dialect, Dari, includes less Arabic and preserves more old words.)

Amir is joking, but the *hadith* (conversation of Mohammed) he quoted is real. I wonder if Amir takes for granted the extreme sexualization of everyday life it implies. If he believes that any two people of the opposite sex will lust after each other if left alone together, sex must have a charge for him that it's lost for most Westerners.

The French anthropologist Germaine Tillion says that in the Mediterranean and Middle East, "We see sexual obsession imposed on men, not just by total separation of the sexes, but also by a sort of etiquette that obliges any boy to pay court to any woman he may find himself alone with." Tillion, writing in what now looks like the lost erotic paradise of 1966 Paris, was scornful of this hypersexualization of everyday life, but I find it charming compared with the studiously gender-neutral attitude of American men.

And when I come back to the house with the chicken, I'm a little disappointed that Shirin and Amir are talking calmly at the table as I left them, not straightening their clothes and buttoning buttons.

As I get to know Amir better, I become convinced that Luisa is wrong about his westernization and decadence. When I offer him wine, he takes only a glass. Smoking seems to be his only vice. It's true that he has more social sophistication than I would have guessed at first. At Princeton he belonged to one of the most prestigious eating clubs, and Shirin says that his Iranian friends are from the oldest families. But religion has a central place in his life that makes him different from most of my friends.

He says he's never doubted the existence of God. A few times he lets it drop that he reads the Quran regularly and once, more shyly, mentions that before he came to Princeton, he prayed five times a day. And when the Muslim fasting month of Ramazan begins just before I leave, Amir proudly tells me that he observes the all-day prohibition on eating, drinking, and smoking. But when I ask him what Ramazan means to him, he can't or won't explain. When I try to dig deeper—*Do you really think the Quran was written by God? Is every word literally true? Why do you drink when that's forbidden? How do you choose what to observe and what to ignore?*—he gracefully dodges the questions.

When Amir and I meet we still just shake hands, but now he calls me *Ann jan*, the way Shirin does. *Jan* literally means "soul," but popularly it means "dear." Like everything else in Farsi, *jan* is ambivalent: not only intimate, what you add to the name of your child, but also, as with the eighteenth-century *goodman*—what you add to the name of your driver.

By the time I leave for Afghanistan, we've become such good friends that Amir joins Shirin at my house just before I go to the airport. He gives me letters he's handwritten in Farsi to Kabul relatives he hasn't seen in decades. With no postal service in Afghanistan, correspondence depends on friends coming and going. And then, watching me fidget with my digital camera, he asks Shirin to take his photo so I can show it to his relatives if I meet them. I have these pictures today. They show an earnest young man, hands clasped in front of him. They also show Amir in my house, rather than his own Brooklyn apartment, which he's told me is small. I am reminded of Afghan jokes about returning exiles who pass around photos of themselves in the United States, standing in front of luxury cars that may or may not actually belong to them.

There's envy in Amir's eyes as we say good-bye, and I wonder if he's thinking about selecting his virgin bride when it's his turn to go. Shirin hugs me tightly, but Amir only shakes my hand, and I feel a flash of disappointment. Perhaps I am falling for his savage Afghan act. There's some artifice to it, but I still find him charming. It's too bad he's so much younger than I am.

It's the age difference more than his belief in arranged marriage that makes me reject out of hand the idea of dating Amir. It's not clear to me that arranged marriages work out worse than the contemporary kind, especially when people marry young. I'm not sure most seventeen-year-olds would make a better choice than their parents would make for them, and in much of the world people still marry young, women often as teenagers.

Arranged marriages were the rule in my own family within

living memory. My mother's father and mother were introduced by a matchmaker, though this might have been because both bride and groom were aged for the time, forty and thirty. My mother's mother's mother, Pesha Gitel, born around 1860, had her husband, Baruch, picked for her. And Baruch's grandparents, born at the beginning of the nineteenth century, were brought together by their families when they were barely thirteen. Of course, those couples, like Afghan couples today, lived with their extended families, and that was part of the glue that made the marriages work.

I've always thought of my own parents' marriage as arranged, though not successfully. They met on a blind date and married a year later, but they never seemed a couple. On some level I must have registered this. When I was very small, I asked my mother if I would have to marry a man named Andy because my parents were named Bernard and Bernice. I was so young I didn't know the difference between first and last names or that married couples had the same name after they got married, but not before. Or maybe I saw that my parents' names were one of their few obvious similarities.

My mother and father had few interests in common, never hugged or kissed in front of me, and didn't seem to have a link to each other besides their respect for each other's intelligence and their role as parents. One time when I described the way they lived in the same house without seeming to be together, my friend Samuel cut to the chase: *You mean they lacked a sense of complicity.* That was right. I never thought of them as having an intimate life of their own behind their bedroom door. When I read Freud in my early twenties, the passionate oedipal jealousies he described didn't register with me. I'd never envied my parents' private life. It wasn't clear they had one. Possibly this has something to do with why I haven't married.

Another reason might be that I haven't found a man who feels like family to me. I understand Amir's desire to marry within his tribe (in his case, literally the same Pashtun subtribe), because I felt the same way until my late thirties. "I'd have more in common with a Jew," I told friends when I was in my twenties and thirties, but I didn't really understand what it was that lovers ought to have in common. I thought of intimacy as based on shared traits and interests, rather than on an emotional connection.

It felt right to me when I just turned nineteen that my first boyfriend, Scott, was Jewish, but at the same time I thought he was too Jewish. I didn't like it that he owned several different yarmulkes, or that he lit Hanukkah candles even in his dorm room. From the start I found his Jewishness not a positive characteristic so much as the absence of a negative, Christianity. Dating a Christian would have raised questions with my family. Although my parents never explicitly told me to marry a Jew, it was understood that I would, just as it was understood that I'd go to an Ivy League college.

Scott and I were together seven years, from the time I was nineteen to twenty-six, but I never saw myself marrying him. Part of the problem, I would have said at the time, was that Scott was too involved with his family. They struck me as stiflingly close; the three adult children still ate Friday night dinner with their parents most weeks. I'd just escaped an unhappy home and didn't wish to immerse myself in someone else's family life, however warm.

And on some sort of primitive chemical level, Scott and his family weren't right for me. I never liked their looks. Scott likely felt something similar. Once he said that I was *awfully dark,* and his tone made me wonder why he was my boyfriend. Not that he wasn't attracted to me—we made love nearly every night we spent together, right till the end—but maybe he didn't want to be. It might have mattered to him that my black hair and eyes and olive skin spoke clearly of Middle Eastern or southern Mediterranean stock. His pale skin and brown hair could have been anything. I thought but never said, *Who knows if they are even really Jewish?* They could only trace their ancestry a few generations back; my mother's father's family was an old rabbinic line, descended from King David. Of course we were *awfully dark.* I didn't identify as Jewish from a religious standpoint, but I was proud of my blood.

Being a member of the tribe, I learned from my years with Scott, didn't make a man feel like family. I wanted someone who looked Jewish but wasn't, and Scott wanted someone who didn't look Jewish but was. He got his wish. He married a pale redhead who converted to Judaism, though I stubbornly refused to think of her as really Jewish. Decades later she finally did something that made me change my mind: She became a rabbi.

Still, for years after Scott, I told people I wanted to marry a Jew. I said so even when I was dating a Catholic or a Protestant. I said so after deciding that I got along better with Christian men than with Jews. I said it after going to Israel and hating it. And my assertion was not so simple as bad faith. Part of me felt that Jews were in some sense better than other people, and Judaism a more reasonable religion—not that I had chosen it. (Shirin thought Amir felt this way about Afghans, and Pashtuns in particular.) Part of me thought it would be easier to marry someone who shared this prejudice. But I knew it was strange for someone who had no religious convictions to care about marrying within the faith. I probably wanted to make a faltering desire true by saying it aloud.

It just so happened that I had trouble getting along with my Jewish boyfriends after Scott. They were defensive and prickly, quarrelsome, critical of me in ways that reminded me of my dad. They were also fussy and wimpy in ways that didn't remind me of my dad, who (whatever his other faults) was physically brave, athletic, and, until he got Parkinson's disease, rugged. I was drawn to Jewish men's dark looks and to something in their presence that reminded me of family, but personality differences always pulled us apart.

I'd wanted to marry a Jew, it now seems to me, because it was a shortcut to the intimacy I had heard belonged to the married state, the intimacy that was missing from my parents' marriage. Amir, oddly enough—or maybe not, since the Pashtuns claim to be descended from King Saul—looked like my family. If I squint, it's Amir who looks back at me from a photo of my mother's father Abe, from his stocky frame to his thick black hair and hooked nose. Amir looks like a Jew but isn't.

Maybe Afghanistan grabbed me the way it did on my first trip because I'd dreamed about going there for almost a quarter century.

It was late August 1978, and I was twenty. At the end of a summer of traveling that had taken Scott and me from Italy to Istanbul, we stood in front of the Magic Bus offices in Sultanahmet. Today the streets are lined with three-dollar-a-cup cappuccino joints and glossy housewares shops, and the area has the feel of one of the better neighborhoods of San Francisco, only with more history. But at that time Sultanahmet was still a stop on the hippie trail, grimy and disreputable, and we were sorry that we couldn't afford to stay elsewhere.

Herat was one of the destinations lettered in a goofy bubble script on the Magic Bus sign. The price was within our almost exhausted means, and we could be in Afghanistan in less than a week. "The *medreseh*," I said to Scott. "The one with the minarets. That's in Herat!" We had not been Harvard students for nothing; we'd read up on our Islamic architecture.

But architecture wasn't what made my heart beat faster when
I read the sign. Afghanistan was the ultimate off-the-beaten-
path destination, grand and dangerous, unspoiled by Harvard
students, or almost; two of Scott's classmates, girls from ancient Boston families, had dined out on their trip to Afghanistan for a couple of years.

I took a step toward the office. Gaunt, aging hippies sat on the
filthy sidewalk smoking suspicious-looking cigarettes. I was
repulsed by the prospect of a trip in close quarters with these
characters, and the feeling was probably mutual. We were two
thin, worried-looking young Americans in worn conservative
clothes, aspiring intellectuals and wannabe bohemians who'd
never stepped outside the confines of the upper middle class.
And for all our collegiate dabbling in pot and LSD, we weren't
in the least present-oriented.

"We can't do it," Scott objected. He was right. If anything went
wrong we'd miss our charter flight back to Boston, and we
didn't have the money for another one. I had to start my senior year in three weeks, and Scott was on his way to a graduate
fellowship at Oxford.

He was right, but we missed our last chance to see Afghanistan
in what Afghans now call the golden years. President Daoud
had been overthrown a few months earlier, in April of 1978,
and political violence would gradually engulf the country.
Daoud's replacement, Taraki, was in turn suffocated in October 1979, and replaced by Hafizullah Amin in another round
of Communist infighting. Finally, on Christmas Eve 1979, the
Soviet army invaded, killing the dangerously independent

Amin. Soon after, the Afghan resistance, which Amir would later fight in, began, and tourism of the sort we had contemplated was finished in Afghanistan.

In the following twenty-four years, I traveled to many other countries, at first with Scott and then with other people, but the time was never right to go to Afghanistan. As time passed my missed opportunity loomed larger. I read every travel book I could find that mentioned Afghanistan. Perhaps because I couldn't go there, I was sure I would have had an amazing trip.

In the meantime, I indulged in a love affair with the Third World. Perhaps because I wasn't sure what my calling was in life, traveling to exotic places became part of how I defined myself. After working on Wall Street as an analyst for twenty months and before beginning Columbia Business School, I took the summer off and went to India for two months. I was alone in small towns and rural areas where I found myself a lonely stranger in a closed society. I made few friends among the Indians. They seemed unable to have a conversation that wasn't an interview, a close questioning as to my education, job, income level, and marital plans. What I loved about India wasn't the humanity, yet the trip was one of the best times of my life up till then. I was spellbound by the magnificence of the art and architecture and by the self-contained nature of Indian society. Things Western seemed irrelevent and remote, and even in 1982 this was a rare—and to me, refreshing—sensation.

When I finished business school in 1984, I was much more excited about my summer travel plans than about the high-paid consulting job I'd spent two years in school to get. I sank my sign-on bonus (all of $5,000) into a four-month trip around the world. I began in Los Angeles, which I'd never seen; I was such an easterner that I'd been to Turkey twice before I went to California. I continued to Hong Kong, Singapore, and then Bali, which at the time was nearly the paradise it's marketed as now. It was almost too much of a paradise; it lacked what I then called "edge." After India, it seemed tame.

And then one morning I stopped on a seven-mile run through the Balinese countryside near Ubud to buy something to drink. It was only eight in the morning but already uncomfortably hot. Since there were no bottled drinks around, I bought some oranges from a gaunt man sitting cross-legged in front of a huge pyramid of fruit.

Bali was cheap then. My hotel room was four dollars, dinner at the pricey place that offered guacamole and chili was two. So I handed the vendor the smallest coin I had, expecting a couple of pieces of fruit. But for a quarter or so, I was handed five or six, far more than I could eat, or, more important, carry while running. Just as I was wondering how to dispose of the extras, an elderly man approached. He spoke sharply to the peddler, who handed me another ten oranges. "He no good, he cheat you," the old man advised.

The picture-postcard paradise of Bali unraveled at that moment. I was entirely sympathetic to the man who had tried to cheat me. If oranges cost little more than a penny apiece, he would only make a couple of dollars when he sold his entire supply. I didn't need fifteen oranges. And I wondered what the people around me ate, and what kind of power they had in their world. It seemed that just by existing, with my American dollars and job, I had entirely too much power over people like this man.

My love affair with the Third World was now tainted, ridden with guilt. But I chose to ignore it. In the next ten years, travel overseas became an occasional indulgence. I was busy making a living and then became absorbed in rock culture and started to publish rock criticism. And for a few years heroin kept me in the East Village, until in 1995 I arranged another long trip to escape it.

In the midnineties, over my drug phase, I turned again to travel, but it was no longer the reason for being it had been in my youth. My identity came from my life and my writing now, not from being someone who traveled. These trips were not as ecstatic as they used to be, and finally, in the poorest place I'd been to in a while—Cuba—I understood why. The trip was not a conventional vacation; I went with Luisa, who had written about Cuba frequently and knew it well, and I published an article, too. It was 1998 and Americans in Cuba were still rare. I soon grew impatient with the language barrier. Maybe because my mother and brother had both majored in Spanish literature, I'd never learned Spanish. I could puzzle out a newspaper from having studied French and Latin, but I had no idea what people were saying. So one day I climbed dozens of white marble steps to the campus of the University of Havana, the oldest in the Western Hemisphere.

I asked about taking Spanish classes. They weren't offered for short-term visitors, the young woman at the reception desk of the office for foreign students explained. Well then, could she recommend some graduate student to me as a private tutor?

She led me to the office of the head of foreign language graduate studies. Carolina was startlingly white and blond in a country that was overwhelmingly black, and middle-aged and sedately dressed in a country where most of the women we tourists saw were twenty-year-old whores in skintight unitards. Carolina said in English that she would be happy to come to my hotel every day to tutor me for two hours a day and suggested the fee of two dollars an hour.

I felt my stomach clench. "No, four dollars an hour, to compensate you for the trouble of transportation," I insisted.

I thought of the Freudian doctrine that the fee for an analysis was part of the treatment, that patients who were treated free would not value their analysis. There was something about paying so little for the lessons that was distasteful, like the ten dollars an hour it cost for hitting with a tennis pro at the Hotel Nacional. That Carolina was ten years older than me and had a high position at the university made it worse. When she came to the government-owned Nacional to give me my first lesson, I ordered us both *café con leche*. The waiter presented the bill, and I nearly sank into the perfectly groomed grass of the courtyard when I saw that it was for four dollars.

I decided then and there that there is such a thing as involuntary sadism. I didn't feel personally responsible for Carolina's poverty. I didn't even think the American embargo was responsible. Castro was. But still I felt like a sadist when I got the bill for that coffee. I felt like a sadist even when I insisted that Carolina take more money for lessons than she'd suggested, and I felt it simply for being able to make such a suggestion. The fact that Carolina's time was worth almost nothing next to an American's was inescapable.

There are inequities—in this case, Castro's oppression of his people by a bankrupt ideology—that make people unable to treat each other as they want to, unable to forget about the immense financial divide between them. And on this trip, this perception was moving from the background to the foreground of my attention.

I was starting to feel that I should keep to the developed world, where most people were on a level. People were nicer in the developing world—there was a warmth and sincerity I loved—but I felt that simply by soaking it up I was doing wrong. It almost made it worse that they had no idea how large the monetary divide between their country and ours was.

My first trip to Afghanistan changed my feelings about the poor countries again. Tied with Sierra Leone for the world's poorest, it was a miserably hard place, by every physical measure, for most of the people who lived there. Still, to my great relief, I did not feel like an oppressor there. I was rich by their standards, but I did not feel they were poor, because they did not feel they were poor. Some of the difference with Cuba and Bali lay in the fact that Afghanistan had never been colonized, some in the famous pride of the Afghans, the self-respect that needed no physical ornament.

Post-Taliban Afghanistan was one of those places that the visitor would think would be depressing, but it wasn't. One crisp November day in Mazar I said to myself, *It's like the morning of the world.* Everything is as if you were doing it for the first time. The hard light and unmodulated colors conspired in the illusion; even ruined apartment blocks or rusted tanks by the side of the road seemed to have been arranged by artful set designers just moments before.

Was the freshness because Afghans experience life directly rather than mediated by television, the Internet, the telephone, and the printed page? (Most Afghan men and nearly all Afghan women are illiterate.) Work, for an increasing number of us in the developed world, is a matter of sitting at a screen and transmitting information and analysis back and forth. Work, in Afghanistan, is negotiating and answering the claims of people face-to-face.

This is not to say that Afghans struck me as more emotionally or gesturally expressive. Their voices were lower and more controlled. When they were tense, they showed it immediately, but by silence and impassive faces. On my first visit, General Dostum's translator confessed to me that when he met large numbers of Americans for the first time during the war, he'd been surprised by their exaggerated gestures and loud voices: *They seem to us like actors in the theater.* And although I didn't think he found me or my friends insincere, I wondered if the flip side of the freshness I saw in Afghans was a staleness they sensed in us.

I didn't think that the Afghans were noble savages, or savages of any kind, despite Jason's witticism about Amir. There were many parts of Afghan culture I didn't like: the iron hand of tradition, unwillingness to take risks, lack of practicality. But since the day I left, I wanted to go back. I needed to feel that sense of the morning of the world again. And I wondered if I would have become a very different person had I gone there in the morning of my life, in 1978, when I was not yet tired of my habits of thought and feeling, when I was only beginning to form them.

I arrive in Mazar for the second time ten days after saying good-bye to Amir and Shirin. It feels like a homecoming of sorts. I recognize Balkh University, lit up at night, as we roll slowly past the gate. The simple, boxlike shapes remind me of my high school; both are distant bastard descendants of the bru-talist architecture of Louis Kahn. But now in mid-November, the trees I remember are bare. Farid, at the wheel, drives with what might seem excessive caution, but I've learned by now that it's necessary. Occasionally an Afghan driver ventures out at night with broken headlights, or turns them off in the Third World belief that it saves money.

Just ahead is a traffic circle and the modern city gates, meet-ing in an arch overhead. But we've gone too far. My traveling companion, Najib, directs Farid to turn around and take a right turn into darkness. We stop at the most basic of shops, a shed with a bare lightbulb casting odd shadows on small piles of vegetables. Farid gets out to ask directions, limping as he walks. He lost part of his right foot to a land mine in the mu-jahideen days, but in the week he's been working for me and

Najib in Kabul, he's always been cheerful and relaxed. Even
now, at the end of twelve hours of driving, he jokes with the
young boy behind the counter. The kid motions to turn left.
The third metal gate on the right is the compound of Nabila
and Abdul Hasib, Najib's first cousins.

Country cousins, he explains, from the rural, Uzbek side of his
family, his father's people. His father had been a rich businessman from a feudal family in another, more remote, province,
Faryab; his mother was a Pashtun aristocrat in Kabul, a cousin
of the king. They lived in Kabul when he was little but visited
Nabila and Abdul Hasib on occasion. Najib hasn't seen his
cousins in eighteen years, because his family fled to the United
States in 1984. Najib is the first to return. Even though he's
an American citizen, he waited a year after the fall of the Taliban, and no one in his family wanted to go with him. I couldn't
understand how anyone who was from Afghanistan wouldn't
want to go back for a visit. I missed the country as soon as
I left it; it must be much worse for Afghans. I understood
Amir's longing to return more than I understood Najib's hes-
itation.

These cousins haven't seen Najib since he was a small boy, and
I have some fears for our reception. What if they don't have
space for us? Nabila and Abdul Hasib don't know me at all. My
only recommendation is that I will be teaching English at
Balkh University and buying books for the university and local
schools. If worst came to worst, I could stay at a hotel, although
it would probably not be good for my reputation at Balkh University to be staying there alone. But Najib reassures me that
his cousins are eager to host us for the next few weeks because
Abdul Hasib was close to his father in their youth.

Farid pounds on the metal gate, and soon it swings back into the darkness. Men are guiding us into a courtyard through a narrow garage nearly filled by a small car. The compound is very large and very dark, and we are led upstairs by flashlight to a series of reception rooms for guests. We finally halt in a room furnished with cushions covered in shades of red and purple and a hodgepodge of enormous new Turkmen rugs in the same colors. I know that traditional Afghan houses don't have Western furniture, but now, standing in this dark room and knowing that I'm going to be living in a house without tables and chairs and box spring mattresses, I feel a rising panic.

Dostum's guesthouse had Western furniture, and until last week I'd been staying at a Kabul guesthouse that reminded me of Dostum's in its casual dirtiness. I interviewed government officials in the morning and ate Indian food every day for lunch, since the Afghan restaurants were closed for lunch during Ramazan. Aside from the fact that I could never get enough hot water to wash my hair and that the Afghan cabinet ministers' offices were warmed by space heaters, I didn't feel that Kabul was all that different from other places I'd been, or from home. But now it hits me all of a sudden just how far away I am. For the first time in Afghanistan I feel a visceral foreignness.

I see an older man in traditional *shalwar kameez,* a green and purple striped Uzbek robe like the one Hamid Karzai has made famous, and a beautifully made grey *karakul* (lambskin) hat. He reaches for the wall, and a bare bulb goes on overhead. I see that he's joined two exposed wires hanging out of the wall. This man is Abdul Hasib, the head of the household.

Squarely built, with the kindly Old Testament face of so many older Afghan men, he doesn't look a bit like Najib, who's tall and skinny, with impossibly thin arms.

With his oddly matched American clothes and stiff posture, Najib looks exactly like the San Jose computer engineer he was until he lost his job in the dot-com collapse. Now he manages a computer store. His father's family is one of the big feudal Uzbek families that have thrown in their lot with Dostum, and Najib is also a Dostum supporter. He'd read some of my articles on Afghanistan and heard about me from Dostum's circle. Just after I returned from my first trip, around the time I met Amir and Shirin, he called me. Perhaps, he suggested, if I wanted to go back to Afghanistan, he would translate for me and help me set up interviews with government ministers. In return I would pay his airfare and some travel expenses.

Suddenly I'm separated from Najib and led back downstairs to another room that's filled with women. There's also one man in his twenties in a black leather jacket over *shalwar kameez.* He's heavyset and surprisingly light skinned, with tightly curled short chestnut hair and brown eyes. Like the other men here, he's clean shaven, generally a sign of secular sympathies in Afghanistan.

"I am Humayon. This is my mother, Nabila, my sisters Banu and Seema and Payman. You will meet my wife and boy and girl five minutes. Rashid is my brother. Please, have tea."

Banu, eighteen or so, hands me a Chinese bowl, and Payman, who looks twelve or thirteen, pours from a metal pot. Seema, short and plump and probably in her midtwenties, smiles but says only, *"khub asteed"*—hello. Like everyone else, the girls are wearing light coats. It's warm tonight for mid-November, but I realize there's no obvious way the house will be heated once winter arrives in full force.

"Khanum, how long have you been married to Najib?" *Khanum* is a Farsi honorific, once used, like the English "Mrs.," for women of good birth and extended to foreign women.

"I ... we ... we are not married. I mean, we are not ... romantically involved at all."

Humayon's face is blank; his English is probably more limited than his initial confidence suggested.

"We are only friends. We work together."

Humayon still looks blank. The Farsi comes to me: *"Maw ham kareem,"* I tell him—we work together. He is puzzled at first by my accent, which is Iranian and bad, but then he seems to understand, and smiles. Humayon might be relieved that his kinsman Najib has not married an infidel after all. He may not be so happy when he sees pictures of Najib's actual wife, a beautiful Hindu from India. Muslim men are allowed to marry Christian and Jewish women, who are also considered people of the book, but not Hindus.

Nabila might be my age or ten years older; it's hard to tell because she is twenty pounds overweight, and the strands of hair escaping her loose beige *chador,* or head scarf, are an obviously dyed pale red-brown. This and the relatively light colors of her clothing—a floor-length dove gray dress topped by a long fuzzy navy and black tweed sweater—proclaim her, by local standards, a political progressive. The women in General Dostum's circle dress this way, and the women in government ministries I'd met in Kabul. Their thin, translucent head scarves are traditionally Afghan, I will eventually learn. The head-to-toe black favored by more conservative women is an import from the Arab countries and postrevolutionary Iran. So is the practice of pinning head scarves in place so that not a hair escapes. Afghan mores are less severe, less formal.

I think Nabila understands English better than she speaks, which is hardly at all. She might be embarrassed to speak, though she holds a highly respected position in Mazar. As Humayon explains, Nabila is the *sar mohallem*, or head teacher, at a local elementary school. This places her among the local female notables in a largely illiterate society that views education with reverence. Seema is also a teacher there. I think I'm misunderstanding her Dari when she says there are 3,160 students at her school, but later when I visit the school, I learn that this is right. Like most provincial schools, they operate on triple sessions.

In comes a tired-looking woman of twenty-two or twenty-three with two small children. Farida, Humayon's wife, is pregnant with their third child. She's about five-eight, robust, and relatively fair in coloring, the ideal Afghan female type, with chestnut hair and skin a few shades lighter than mine. Like all the other women, she wears what looks in the dim light to be layers of shapeless long dresses topped by a sweater; a head scarf of gray polyester is draped around her head. She smiles shyly.

Her children, Loulou and Siddiq, big and healthy looking for three and five, are friendlier and less sulky than most American kids their age. Loulou skips right up to me and Najib, barefoot, in a little pink jumpsuit. Her tiny face is broad, Central Asian, her skin tawnier than her parents', and her hair is as dark as mine. We kiss hello, and I ask Loulou if she has a pet.

"*Gosfand,*" she says, a sheep. The adults laugh.

The next thing I know, everyone is turning in for the night. Najib, as a relative, will sleep here in the *khaneh,* a word for "house" that's also used for the main eating and socializing room. I realize that besides Banu and Nabila and Abdul Hasib, who have rooms off the *khaneh,* no one has a fixed bedroom in the Western sense, just as there are no beds. They all make little nests for themselves among the hard red pillows, pulling thick new flowered polyester blankets from stacks in the corners. After a bit of consultation between Nabila and Najib, I'm led back upstairs to one of the large, drafty reception rooms we passed through earlier.

In Afghan family compounds, I've read, the guest room or suite is always above the front door, in an intermediate position between inside and out. Guests are to be honored, but they also carry a threat. I am amused to be living what had been anthropological lore to me until now. I recall that the toilet, another place of ambiguous purity, is also usually near the front door, and I'm glad to see that this is the case here, too, because the bathroom adjoining my room has a cold-water shower, but no toilet.

As I stack a few of the large cushions one upon the other and place my sleeping bag atop that, I remember my childhood picture book of "The Princess and the Pea." I also notice how impractical the room is. The curtains are thin lace and do nothing to protect the room from the drafts that flow through the poorly sealed windows. The only artificial light is from a dim bulb in the center of the ceiling, far too distant from the cushions that border the room to help with reading. But so far I have not seen any books in this house, either. I look at my alarm clock and it is only nine-thirty, but I'm exhausted by the effort of speaking Farsi and adjusting to the new surroundings. I reach for the exposed wires and gingerly pull them apart to turn out the light. There are no house lights from any other part of the compound visible through the window, and the street outside is equally dark.

The next morning Najib and I share an infidel's breakfast of pomegranate seeds, hard-boiled eggs, and green tea with the children. Najib says he's not religious, but all the other adults took their breakfast before dawn and won't eat till sundown. (Children under eleven aren't supposed to fast.) At breakfast I talk a little with Rashid, Humayon's younger brother, a doctor and still unmarried at the ripe age of twenty-four. He's much darker than Humayon but similar in build, and his English isn't bad. He tells me that they have a treat for me and Najib, and soon Banu brings it into the room: a canteloupe. "From U.S.," Rashid assures me. He translates for the American soldiers protecting the Jordanian Field Hospital in Mazar, and they've given him some of their extra fruit, flown in from the United States to this country, famous from antiquity for its melons.

While I'm still eating, Loulou runs through the courtyard, still barefoot in the late fall cold, calling *gosfand!* I grab my digital camera and hasten to meet her pet. Nabila and Humayon and Banu and Siddiq and Loulou gather for a photograph with the sheep, which, disconcertingly, is on a rope. Najib catches my eye and says sotto voce, "You may not want to watch this." And then Humayon pulls the sheep over to a small trench in the concrete entranceway, just outside the bathroom, and slits its throat according to the principles of halal slaughter, which, like kosher slaughter, aims to minimize the animal's fear and pain. I have to look away and I feel like a weakling. The sheep, I realize, was bought and killed in honor of us guests. Loulou does not seem at all upset, and I realize she has no idea of a pet in our sense; animals are for food in her world. I have a pretty good idea of what we'll be having for dinner.

That first dinner blurs in memory with many others. For everyone except Najib and me and the children, it breaks the day's fast. Although the dark comes early now, around five fifteen, it's still been thirteen hours since their last meal. We sit on the cushions against the walls of the *khaneh,* under a single lightbulb. The room is warmed more in theory than in practice by a space heater plugged first into a frayed extension cord and then into an ungrounded outlet. The green plaster walls are dotted here and there with framed family photos, but otherwise there is no decoration but the thick red Turkmen carpets on the floor. In one corner there's a TV and VCR; the family, I'll learn, loves Indian movies like everyone else here.

A feast is laid out on a plastic tablecloth that covers the carpets: *salatah* of chopped parsley, tomatoes, onions, and cucumbers; chopped spinach; fresh Uzbek naan or flatbread; bowls of *manti,* or Uzbek meat dumplings in a thick pool of oil, topped with yoghurt and dried mint sauce; a giant plate of *pilau* studded with mutton chunks from the slaughtered sheep. I'm surprised there isn't more meat, but Najib explains that most is given to the poor. Aside from the bottles of Fanta and Coke and the bowls of hard candies from Uzbekistan that punctuate the display, there's no manufactured food at all. The food is delicious, though some of it is cooked with too much oil for my taste, and I eat everything with no ill effects.

Najib and I usually sit *bala,* or at the head of the room, in the place of honored guests, except when Nabila's aunt Gulnora comes to visit. The withered but lively eighty-year-old woman is visiting from her home a day's drive away in Maimana. After hearing so much about the oppression of Afghan women, I'm stunned not only that she sits *bala* but also that she is the only person I ever see smoking in the house. In Afghan society, one doesn't smoke in front of one's social superiors, and because most socializing takes place among family groups rather than peers, few people smoke at all. I didn't know Afghan women ever did. But Gulnora is honored not only for her age and her status as a large landowner but because her late husband, Najib's father's brother, was a major political figure among the Uzbeks of northern Afghanistan. He was an intellectual who drew attention to ethnic Uzbek culture and founded a cultural movement later taken over by General Dostum and turned into a political party.

The night Gulnora arrives, I hear something that puzzles me. She seems to be the aunt of both Abdul Hasib and Nabila, and I think I've misunderstood. But no, Najib explains, a bit embarrassed, Abdul Hasib and Nabila are first cousins. Farida and Humayon are also related, he explains, though more distantly.

I've read in anthropology books that in Afghanistan, as well as in many other traditional Islamic societies, marriage to the paternal first cousin is preferred. This custom extends from high to low, but it's especially favored in landowning families like this one because it keeps the property in the family. (Najib's parents are not related—are in fact of different ethnic groups—but theirs was another sort of bargain: Najib's father's wealth for the royal descent of his mother.)

Cousin marriage is a pre-Islamic tradition, one Mohammed did not support, because it reinforces tribal rather than religious ties. For Mohammed, the Islamic community was meant to be the strongest bond, and many of his injunctions about family law in the Quran went directly contrary to Arabian tribal practice. As Germaine Tillion has noted, these are the Quranic precepts that tend to be ignored by many Muslims today—the right of women to inherit property and to control their dowries—while ancient customs never mentioned in the Quran, such as male circumcision, are universal in Islam.

This household is traditional in other ways. While Nabila eats in leisure with the men, the junior women, Farida and Banu and Payman, cook and serve and clean up, sitting down with the men and us older women only at the end of the meal. (Seema falls in between, pitching in on occasion but exempt from the heavier work, perhaps because of her teaching job.) The system doesn't offend me, because it's based on age as much as gender, and I'm pleased that here a woman gains in status as she ages. Women over forty or so are treated more like men in Afghan society, with more freedom of movement and behavior, as well as more respect. Their situation is closer to that of women in the West, and so I fit more comfortably into the society than I would have at twenty, had I actually made it onto that Magic Bus to Herat.

I'm curious about everything around me and puzzled by much of it, but I don't ask as many questions as I would have expected. I don't talk that much. For one of the few times in my life, I just experience my surroundings. Part of the reason is a conscious decision to try to live this life without judging. But part of the reason is that I'm happy. Much to my surprise, I've felt among friends from the start. The affection that radiates from the family, especially Nabila and Loulou and Siddiq, is more intense than anything I've felt from my own family. It more than compensates for the undeniable annoyances and discomforts of this life, the lack of hot water, heat, and privacy.

I probably spend so much time playing with the children because it's easier than trying to frame grammatical sentences for the grown-ups. I'm less likely to commit a blunder in etiquette as well. But they are open and affectionate, as happy children are, and I relish our time together.

Loulou and Siddiq are always with us in the *khaneh* during dinner and after, passed from one lap to the next, hugged by a great-aunt, a cousin, an uncle. They sometimes talk with one relative or another or with each other, but they're mainly seen and not heard. Eventually they fall asleep in someone's lap, and Farida comes to take them to the room they sometimes share with her and Humayon, or they just spend the night in the *khaneh*. It's nothing like the elaborate bedtime rituals I remember from my childhood and see with my friends' children in New York. I think my lifelong insomnia—a common American affliction—stems from these pre-bedtime hours of anxiety. The fear I felt then might have been a fear of death or of being alone, and American child-rearing practices take it for granted. Here it doesn't seem to exist, and I wonder why.

I'm also surprised that Loulou and Siddiq don't fight. Granted, my brother and I were much farther apart in age—six years, not two—but we bickered constantly. So did most brothers and sisters I remember from my childhood, or see in my friends' homes now in America.

My brother was born when I was a few months shy of six. He'd been much wanted, except, psychoanalytic wisdom suggests, by me. I remember an odd episode from when I was six or seven. I'd begun to collect erasers that I found at school, the sort that we would fit over the ends of our pencils when we had used up the erasers they came with. It wasn't so often that a child dropped one, but whenever I saw one, I picked it up. When my mother asked me why I had a collection of dirty little erasers, I couldn't explain. But I remember very clearly that I wanted to save them from being thrown away. I saved them not because I found them enticing but because no one else did. I kept them out of a misplaced (a psychoanalyst would say *displaced*) sense of compassion. And what would that have been a displacement of? Who did I want to save, and from what? Or whom did I feel guilty about not wanting to save?

I wanted to tell my parents to take my brother back where they'd got him, send him away, throw him out. He was small and pink and fragile, like the erasers. And because I wished he were as unwanted as they were, while also feeling guilty about wanting to throw him out, I symbolically rescued him. But because I acted out only the rescue and not the discarding, I also found a rescuing that would annoy my mother and thus bring down a milder form of the punishment I felt I deserved for my thoughts.

During my childhood, my brother and I never really became friends. The nearly six-year age difference had something to do with that. Loulou and Siddiq are close enough in age to play together. But part of it has to do with cultural expectations. My parents expected sibling rivalry—all the Freudian-influenced baby books told them it was normal. They were also brought up in a Jewish American subculture that encouraged frankness, informality, and open airing of conflict. Afghan culture is very different.

"They are taught to call each other *sh'ma*," Nabila tells me through Humayon. *Sh'ma* is the formal "you" in Persian, the sign of respect—not only Loulou to her *lala* (older brother) but also Siddiq to Loulou. I know that a girl in Afghanistan would defer to her older brother, but I am surprised that they would also tell Siddiq to call Loulou *sh'ma*. Maybe Afghan society isn't as sexist as the stereotypes have it.

This society, maligned in America as unenlightened, seems to have better ways of raising children, at least small children, than we do. Of course there is a price to pay for this tranquillity and warmth. Loulou and Siddiq play only with each other; and they know very little of the world, even their local world, compared to American children of their age. Afghan kids don't have play dates, and they socialize only with their relatives. I've also read, though not seen, that Afghan infants are

quieted with opium, that toddlers are discouraged from asking questions. When I give Humayon a picture book for Loulou and Siddiq, he's uncertain what to do with it; he's never
read them a book in their lives and likely never will. This is the
first book either child has ever owned; by five, like most kids
of my background, I had a shelf full of children's books.

And yet Loulou and Siddiq are unusually bright and curious.
Siddiq is charming and quick; he loves tinkering with the
Western technology I bring into the house. I have to tell his
parents that it's okay if he tries typing on my computer or taking a picture with my camera; they're afraid he will break the
equivalent of a Rolls-Royce.

Loulou is my favorite. She's just turned three, bubbly and outgoing and physically tough, like the 60 percent of Afghan kids
who will make it to age five. Remarkably bright and observant,
she takes her first photo with my digital camera almost un-
aided. Later, she shows me an ad in one of the *National Geo-
graphic*s I've brought over. It's for a battery recharger like the
one she's seen me fiddle around with every night when the
power comes on for a few hours. Loulou is also a natural per-
former. When there are visitors, which is most nights now during Ramazan, she's often called upon to dance for her elders
to a crackly Uzbek tape on the family boom box.

Some time into my stay I realize Loulou and Siddiq don't have
any toys. My first reaction is to buy them a tricycle. I intend it
more for Loulou—as a boy Siddiq will have more opportunities for exercise as soon as he starts school. But they both ride
it around the courtyard. I wonder what other gifts might be
good. I still remember the toys of my childhood: the little

Wedgwood blue and white plastic desk, the dollhouse my
father built me, the beige Lego castle, really my brother's. My
brother and I had always had a lot of toys, perhaps because
when my mother was growing up, she felt deprived. She and I
talked about it just before I left for Afghanistan.

"I only had one doll, and all the other kids had more. That's
why you had a Barbie when you were three."

"When I was three? What was I doing with a Barbie when I
was three?"

"The little girl next door you used to play with had one."

Looking at Loulou, I was horrified to think of her playing with
a Barbie. I was horrified to think of me playing with a Barbie
at that age. But I understood what my mother was trying to
do. We were supposed to be modern American children, full
participants in the consumer society she had felt excluded
from. My mother's family rebelled against the same traditional world that I was drawn to. My mother's father, Abe,
whom she hated bitterly, was the first rebel in her family, drop-
ping out of yeshiva to become a carpenter and immigrate to
America, where he was briefly a successful real estate devel-
oper. Abe not only refused to become a rabbi like his ancestors but turned stubbornly irreligious. He didn't go to shul or
keep kosher. These were drastic steps. He was only a few generations removed from ancestors who had presided over a rab-
binical court.

Abe and his wife, Becky, my mother's mother, had been born
in small towns in Belarus, and they hadn't had any toys, ei-

ther. Like Loulou and Siddiq, they'd grown up in large families of eight or ten children. They had never been alone. When my mother was small, Abe had been rich; if she didn't have toys it wasn't because of a lack of money. It simply hadn't occurred to her parents—I now think—that toys were what childhood happiness was made of.

The problem, though, was that Abe and Becky were too unhappy themselves to provide the warmth that surrounded Loulou and Siddiq. According to my mother, her parents were depressed, and her father was mean and selfish. She didn't like them and didn't talk with her father in the last years of his life. He never saw me, though I was born two years before he died. But unlike my mother, I didn't believe that adopting American ways was the answer, either. I felt lonely much of my childhood, despite the many toys I had to keep me company. Loulou and Siddiq have the happy confidence of children who have always been surrounded by love and easy intimacy. They have no toys, yet they're the least needy kids I've ever known. I decided that buying them toys wouldn't necessarily be doing them a favor.

Instead, I talk with Humayon and Farida and Nabila about taking Loulou to New York for a year. I dream of helping her become bilingual, exposing her to selected American ways, grooming her to be the first woman president of her country (and Afghanistan might just have a woman president before we do). To my surprise, everyone likes the thought, though on reflection we all think a few months is a better idea than a year. But I'm afraid her spirit would wither in the thinner air of my city, that my love and the attentions of my friends would not begin to compensate for the absence of her parents and aunts and uncle and grandparents who all live with her here. I'm both disappointed and relieved to learn that until the American Embassy in Kabul opens a visa section, it's very unlikely Loulou will be visiting me.

But I promise to return as soon as I can, and I mean it. Despite the many ways this life grates on me, it's offered me a vision of family life as more than a zero-sum game. I know that I'm supposed to be able to take this insight and apply it to my own life in New York, but I'm not optimistic about the chances of this happening. It's enough for me that this other world exists and that I can return to it.

6 | *fifty years are not enough*

For two weeks in Mazar, I settle into a routine. I spend the mornings studying Farsi, playing with Loulou and Siddiq, and buying school supplies for Nabila's school or Balkh University. I've been using what I can afford from my own money and funds from my friend Maud to buy dictionaries and photocopy old English grammar books for the Balkh University English department's two hundred students. Then I eat a very light lunch—not so much in deference to Ramazan as because of the scarcity of bathrooms at Balkh—and go to teach English from one to four. After that, I check my e-mail (I've befriended the Nigerian consultant who keeps the servers running at the public phone center, and he lets me use his computer). Then it's dusk and time to head home for the breaking of the fast. Dinner is finished by six thirty, and by nine thirty or ten, I'm in bed.

As my stay draws to a close, the charm of traditional Afghan provincial life is wearing off. I don't feel that I'm getting enough done, the lack of exercise is making me antsy, and it's growing ominously colder at night. Now I'm wearing two sweaters in my three-season down sleeping bag, and I'm still having trouble falling asleep. The Afghan winter, I've heard, begins abruptly in December and is as fierce as New England's, though not as long.

As December approaches, the talk in the family and at Balkh University is all of Eid, the three-day holiday that brings the fasting month of Ramazan to a close. Ramazan is supposed to end at sundown on December 5, but because Islamic holidays are based on the lunar calendar, the exact timing depends on the mullahs in Saudi Arabia sighting the new moon over Mecca. Balkh University will be closed for vacation for a week. My last day of teaching is November 30, and my flight from Kabul to Dubai is December 7, so I have some time to see more of Afghanistan.

Not much happens just before and during Eid—it's like Christmas at home. I planned to go to Herat this trip, and a government minister in Kabul even offered to introduce me to Ismail Khan, the self-appointed governor of Herat Province. But I'd stayed in Mazar too long, choosing family life over political interviews. So when Nabila suggests going to her hometown, Maimana, on December 1 and staying for the beginning of the holiday, I consider it. Maimana is the capital of Faryab Province, an agricultural area along the Turkmen and Uzbek border in Afghanistan's northwest. Maimana isn't known for much of anything. It's poor, Nabila admits, but beautiful. Looking at the map, I see that Maimana is a third of the way from Mazar to Herat. Maybe I can just continue on and reach Herat before Eid. But everyone agrees it's too dangerous. There are bandits on the stretch between Maimana and Herat, and travelers have been robbed and killed. So Herat will once more have to wait.

I console myself that the trip from Mazar to Maimana will be something of an adventure. After two hours on a well-paved, two-lane highway to Sheberghan (Dostum's headquarters, where I stayed on my first trip), there's a long stretch through the desert with no real road, just dozens of crisscrossing car tracks. And I'm curious about Maimana. Nabila claims it was an enlightened place when she was growing up in the sixties. In the photo albums that show her as a teenager with her cousins, the girls are wearing miniskirts, sometimes with head scarves. Then, too, I'd already spent a few mornings going with Humayon and Abdul Hasib to the bazaar to buy supplies for the pitifully underequipped Maimana schools, and I might as well see where my money is going.

Oddly, only Najib is coming with us. Maimana is the home-town of his father, too, and he's related to everyone from the governor on down. None of the others want to go, and Loulou and Siddiq are deemed too little for the trip. Instead, some cousins from Sheberghan will join our party. We will be so many that Nabila hires a Hiace minivan, along with a driver.

The night before we leave, we go to Farida's parents' com-pound in a different part of Mazar for a big dinner. Farida's brother Kamran shows me the artifacts he's found in the Ark, or citadel, of Balkh—known in antiquity as Bactria, the an-cient ruined city supposedly built by Alexander the Great near present-day Mazar. There are some amazing medieval bowls, but none is whole; even the biggest are composed of dozens of pottery fragments. I picked up many pieces like these myself when Humayon took me and Siddiq there one afternoon. But Kamran has some with calligraphy on them. Seeing my admiration, he tells me to take something. He offers some of the patched-together bowls. I eye them greedily but take a piece that I know has no commercial value, a fragment that seems to come from the bottom of a small plate. "That's the name of the Prophet," Humayon comments. And it looks like it says "Mohammed"; reading ornamental calligraphy is hard for me. I can ask Shirin or Amir what they think when I get home.

The next morning we set out at dawn for Maimana. After Sheberghan, where ten of Nabila's cousins fill the car to capacity, we enter the scrublands of the Dasht-e-Leila. The desolate beauty of the golden grasslands is broken occasionally by a cluster of perfunctory mud brick huts and black goatskin tents. The only inhabitants are Kuchi nomads, an ethnic group of mysterious origins. The Dasht-e-Leila isn't a desert at all, but rich pasturelands. That's why the nomads are here. I become restive when the driver keeps insisting on how easy it is to get lost and wander around forever in the Dasht-e-Leila.

"No, if you have a compass, you won't get lost. And you can just see from the sun which way to go," I point out crossly. Sometimes Afghans seem to have no common sense. Or perhaps this is a Cultural Difference. I grew up playing in deep woods and have spent a lot of time trekking and hiking all over the world. Like many Americans, I'm at home in the outdoors, and these rolling grasslands strike me as one of the least dangerous places I've been in Afghanistan. Yet everyone else finds it scary. And what they take for granted—our driving at a precipitous angle over ruts—is what makes me nervous.

When I tell our driver that I have a Nissan in New York, he insists that I take the wheel to prove it. Driving is not part of the ordinary Afghan's skill set; even many people rich enough to own cars don't know how to drive them. And women don't drive at all, though there's no law against it—only custom. When I showed my Balkh students my driver's license and credit card by way of a practical English lesson, they were less surprised by the unfamiliar notion of credit, or by a skill set legally required for driving, than by the fact that I was "allowed" to drive in my culture. So as much to make a point about American society as anything else, I take a turn on the network of car tracks that is our road. The Hiace is an amazing car, capable of driving at a nearly 45-degree angle, as I have to here, but I don't want to push my luck. I give the wheel back to the driver after a few hundred yards.

When we finally enter inhabited areas again in the market town of Daulatabad, I'm charmed to see horse carts and boys on camelback. It's market day, and vendors have arranged their crude wooden carts of fruit and vegetables around the *maidan,* the central oval ringed by the tiny bazaar. The shops are whitewashed and blue-shuttered and utterly adorable. Heaps of taxi-yellow carrots and fiery red tomatoes are piled on the carts, along with onions, garlic, and leeks. There are scarcely any manufactured goods offered here, and those, like jars of green hot sauce and tiny coarse wool tunics for little boys, seem to have been made locally. We park next to the only four cars in town. Everyone else has arrived on horseback or on foot. The locals stare at us when we climb out to look around, not because of me, for once, but because Najib and the other men of our party are wearing citified leather jackets

over their *shalwar kameez*. There are no other women in the
market. In Afghanistan, food shopping is done by men so
women don't have to speak with unrelated men.

This is the real Afghanistan, I tell myself, and try to snap some
pictures, but my camera batteries have died. The strange and
wavering current in Nabila's house never charged them fully. I
look around, intent on remembering. I feel that in my lifetime
this will all change.

But when we drive into Maimana just before sunset, my heart
sinks. It's the provincial capital, but it looks like a hellhole.
What was charming in a village is numbing in a town of thirty-
five thousand. The horse and wagon teams that seemed so
quaint en route are depressing when they turn out to be the
only taxis. The streets are foot-deep rutted mud. The hundreds
of shops are tiny wooden hovels with wooden doors instead of
windows, and almost all of them offer the same miscellany of
archaic goods—foot-pedal-operated sewing machines, irons
that have to be heated in the fire, simple handmade axes and
saws. Except for the cheap polyester clothing from Pakistan,
this could be an American frontier town circa 1880.

The compound of Nabila and Najib's aunt and uncle, Amina
and Enayatullah, also feels like something out of another century. It's huge—the inside courtyard must be half an acre—but
stone cold. There's only a pump and a well in the courtyard,
no running water, and the toilet is a perfect rectangle of
packed earth. It's immaculate, but it's still dirt. There is elec-
tric light in only a few rooms, and only because the family has
a generator; Maimana has an ongoing electricity shortage.
Only one room used in the daytime has anything like heating.

There, a lucky half dozen people can drape themselves around the *sandali*—the Central Asian stove, which consists of carpets covering a box of hot coals. At night I feed a tiny wood-burning stove in my room until I get warm enough to fall asleep, but the cracks in the windows and the poorly fitted door ensure that my room never becomes comfortable. When I wake, the thermometer on my alarm clock reads thirty-seven degrees Fahrenheit; the wind is whistling through the gap between the window and the wall. I can't understand why the family doesn't insulate the rooms better, especially as firewood isn't plentiful or cheap.

There's a reason for me to be here: I bought supplies for the schools, though they're closed now in anticipation of Eid. But I'm coming to the conclusion that it's much easier to enjoy helping the poor when you don't have to live like them.

The night we arrive, Mahmoud, one of the men of the house, a thirty-year-old engineer who speaks English, introduces me to his wife, Nailya. She's a tall, big-boned, good-looking girl, and I see that she's well into a pregnancy. "I married her a year ago," Mahmoud says. "She was fifteen then. I'm very lucky." And he smiles at me; it's obvious that he is referring to her youthful good looks. Then he explains that Nailya is also his first cousin.

Mahmoud claims that Nailya knows a little English but that she's too shy to speak. I feel sorry for her. There were a lot of marriages of young girls during the Taliban period because families figured that if girls couldn't go to school, they'd be better off getting started on their career of motherhood. Nailya probably didn't go to school after 1997, when the Taliban took Dostum's territory. This would mean she finished fifth grade.

Nailya's formal education is over now. Instead, she's embarked on a life of hard work. While Nabila's house has running water, here all the family's water is hand pumped by the women. They also bake bread daily, while Humayon bought the bread we ate in Mazar. And milk and *chaka* (a sour loose cheese with the texture of ricotta) come from the cow in the muddy far reaches of the courtyard.

"How many people live here?" I ask Enayatullah over dinner.

"I don't even know." He laughs. "Maybe forty?"

It must be a vast amount of labor just to put meals on the table, I think.

Later Mahmoud asks me how much it costs to get a wife in America. "We don't buy our wives in America," I answer with an air of superiority. I remember Amir's approval of the Afghan tradition of paying a bride-price. "Men and women are both able to make their livings. They marry for love, when they have enough money to set up a home together." But as I boast of our advanced society, other less-than-ideal aspects of American courtship and marriage come to mind: the relentless emphasis on male earning power as translated into sexual appeal, unhappy couples dragging their kids through malls, the astonishing divorce rate. I don't want Mahmoud to know how unhappy we often are, but I would still choose that over adolescent marriages and bride-prices. And my gorge rises when I think of Amir's wish for a seventeen-year-old bride— just a year older than Nailya. He'd be marrying a fifth grader. Why had I defended him?

I've just about decided that these people—immensely hospitable and kind and warm as they are—are also impenetrably different, irredeemably savage. And then Najib catches my eye. "Did you hear what my aunt Gulnora just said? That's an Uzbek saying. It is something that an old man is telling his wife. 'I hope that we meet in the afterlife, because fifty years together are not enough.'"

I want to weep. I can't find a man I can love for more than a few years, and these people think fifty are not enough. My mother told me recently that she never loved my father and felt that he never really loved her. What had their free choice availed them? I feel again here, in the mud and boredom of Maimana, what I had also seen in family life in Mazar: the hint of a vanished tenderness between men and women that survives, with Americans, only in the bedroom, and rarely there. And I notice how Nailya's eyes are always on Mahmoud, even though she stands in the shadows with the adolescent daughters of the house as he sits with the other adult men.

Still, despite this epiphany, I return gratefully to Mazar two days later. Abdul Hasib is amused at my speedy reappearance, and Banu simply says, "There is nothing to do in Maimana. That's why I didn't go." Perversely it's even colder here than in Maimana, because the local government, Mohammed Atta's, ran out of money to pay for the electricity they buy from Uzbekistan. The power has been out for days, snow is on the ground, and the generator and the car are both broken at the house. Still, the family is here, and I spend a last night with them around the *sandali,* now set up in Humayon and Farida's room. Everyone but me is sleeping here, all three generations;

I wonder how Humayon and Farida manage to have sex. I go back up to my room, and it's so cold that my PowerBook stops working when I try to turn it on to take notes. I take it into my sleeping bag with me to keep it alive.

My last day in Mazar, I wake up in a frigid room and wash my face with water so cold it leaves me breathless. *Thank God I'll be in Kabul tonight, with a shower and a heated bedroom,* I tell myself. I'll even be able to wash my clothes, rather than just reversing them when they get dirty. I contemplate the snow-covered courtyard and tell Humayon that I'll shovel the pathways if he shows me where the shovel is, and when he tells me they don't have a shovel, I nearly explode. "Why don't you own a snow shovel," I ask, "when it snows here every winter?" Then I realize how badly my temper is deteriorating. Part of the problem is that I haven't eaten anything this morning and I only had one meal the day before, because I was in cars all day returning from Maimana to Mazar. I feel that I'm not thinking clearly.

I hear a deep rumbling all around me in the courtyard, a noise at first unfamiliar.

"Your plane," Humayon explains. There's no regular commercial air service from Mazar to anywhere, but Abdul Hasib read in the paper that the government has organized a special flight to take people to Kabul for Eid. It's arriving now, and we head for the airport outside town.

As usual in Afghanistan, urgency is misplaced. It's four hours before I get on the plane. Humayon waits with me for an hour and learns that the real rationale for the flight is the visit of the Kabul-based Minister of Civil Aviation, Mir Wais Sadiq, to meet with officials here to discuss expanding air service to Mazar. Mir Wais is the son of Ismail Khan, Herat's governor. But Mir Wais and his delegation have now gone to visit friends and do Eid shopping in Mazar. The airport is unheated, and there's no food available—whether because it's Ramazan or not, I don't know. I tell Humayon that he might as well leave. A few hours later, he's back, along with his father, who seems to magically know when the plane will actually go.

I commit a terrible breach of decorum by planting a farewell kiss on Abdul Hasib's cheek, and I board the plane with a full heart. I will miss Loulou and Siddiq, and when I tell them I love them, words they understand in English, I mean it. Siddiq has a boy's embarrassment at emotion, but Loulou is tearful as we say good-bye. So am I; she's the only person in a long, long time who has loved me for my heart, not my body or my mind.

After twenty minutes in the air I notice an unbroken rise of mountains below us as far as I can see, impossibly jagged and uninhabitable looking. They don't resemble anything I remember from the trip from Kabul to Mazar. The steward (internal Ariana flights do not have women working on board) admits that the plane is stopping in Herat, before continuing on to Kabul. Now the rationale behind the rationale appears: Mir Wais Sadiq is going home to Herat for Eid and taking a few dozen of his closest pals with him.

My mind is working slowly because I've hardly eaten in twenty-four hours, but the thought of Herat penetrates my fog. Maybe I can get there after all. Maybe I should try to approach Mir Wais and see if I can get a meeting with his father. I think about walking to the front of the plane. But Eid is about to start, and the year's biggest family holiday seems an insensitive time to request an interview. I stay in my seat. (Mir Wais was later killed in factional fighting in Herat in March 2004, illustrating the adage that there's no time like the present for meeting an Afghan cabinet minister.)

As the wintry mountain landscape below gives way first to desert and then to sunny farmland, I see what look like ancient buildings underneath and remember the *medreseh* with the minarets. Finally I'm getting a glimpse of the city that Magic Bus trip had promised in 1978. As we circle and land, I think once more about getting off. But then I look out the window. There are far more people waiting on the tarmac than there are available seats on our plane, even if everyone who came from Kabul and Mazar were to leave. With all the Eid travelers, I might not be able to get on a plane out of Herat in time to make my flight from Kabul to Dubai in a few days. After spending more than I'd planned on supplies for schools, I'm down to just a few hundred dollars. There are no branches of American banks in Kabul (not to mention ATMs), and the hotels don't take credit cards. My situation reminds me of Scott's objections in Istanbul to the Magic Bus trip.

I assume many of those people on the tarmac—the women all in *chad'ris*—will be turned around and sent home. But no. They're all allowed to board the plane. Three cheerful men clutching plastic bags of Eid candies and dried fruit see the exit row and crouch on suitcases at my feet, while the aisles fill with men standing up, holding on to the baggage compartments like straphangers on the subway at home. Now I know staying on board was the right decision.

At Kabul airport, many of the women in *chad'ris* finally take them off. So they weren't very conservative, just following local custom or pressures. As soon as I enter the baggage claim area, I hear a familiar voice. It's Farid, my driver in Kabul who took me and Najib to Nabila's house in Mazar. He looks for clients on each incoming flight, so it's not such a coincidence. We walk to his car together, and I adjust my pace to his slower one. And as we get in his car, I utter the words I've been rehearsing in Farsi for the last few days, relishing the sensations of running water, a hot shower, a heated room: "Please take me to the InterContinental."

I close the door to my room and I'm truly alone for the first time in Afghanistan. It feels odd. I turn on the space heater—the hotel's electricity comes from its own generator and isn't sufficient to power the central heating of old—dash to the bathroom and turn on the shower. There is indeed hot water. But by the time I peel off my five layers of filthy clothes, it is cold. The bathroom is freezing and I wash as best I can. Then, trying to dry myself as quickly as possible with the frayed, abrasive towel—judging from its shade of yellow, part of the original seventies décor—I look at my naked body in the mirror. There were no floor-length mirrors anywhere I stayed in Kabul or Mazar or Maimana. I haven't seen my body's reflection since I left Dubai, and what I see shocks me. I've lost ten pounds easily, but I don't look very healthy. Or maybe it's that I've forgotten how to look at my body in the mirror. Maybe I have forgotten how to see nakedness as sensual and erotic. My body just looks vulnerable and fragile. I remember that I'm now free to pick up a man and take him back to my room. It can't be very difficult, given the high male-female ratio I noticed my first week here. But I can't quite run the scenario through. It seems to belong to another place and another person.

Although I longed for occasional privacy when I was with Nabila's family, I've fallen out of the habit of being alone. I spend the next few days in Kabul with one or another person I chance upon—an American mine-removal expert, an older American woman I met on my first stay here, a young Afghan journalist. I'm experiencing withdrawal from the closeness of family life, and it's both liberating and lonely. It's great to be speaking English with native speakers again and having conversations I can't have with anyone in Mazar, but I realize this doesn't mean that we have an emotional connection. Even as I count the days until I can lie on the beach in Dubai, I feel the pull of staying longer.

I think about a conversation I had in Maimana with Mahmoud and two of his cousins. They were showing me family photo albums by the light of a kerosene lamp. In the photos, Mahmoud and his family pose stiffly in front of tall buildings in Karachi. Mahmoud said he'd enjoyed some things about life in a city with electricity and cinemas and tall buildings, but not others, and his family had never thought of staying there. "This is our home," he stated firmly. And in Kabul I began to understand that this wasn't just an expression of national pride or nostalgia. Mahmoud and his family love Afghanistan with the same visceral, unconditional affection parents feel for their children. Afghanistan's frailty calls forth the love of its people, just as children's vulnerability calls forth parental love. "The strength of weakness," in the words of the reactionary nineteenth-century American writer George Fitzhugh.

Weakness hadn't been a quality I've responded to much in my life. Maybe this is because my father was diagnosed with Parkinson's disease when I was ten. I steeled myself against the horror of his deterioration and, by extension, against weakness in general. I ran the Boston Marathon in college and plunged into obsessions with different sports—martial arts, surfing, tennis—and with staying fit. I hated sickness in myself and others; I stayed away from the ill and the frail.

But I was also drawn to the very situations that scared me. I played with illness in the form of heroin addiction for years, a sham, artificial vulnerability that was really another form of imperviousness—or was it the other way around? And then there was my travel to poor countries and my revulsion at what felt like the Western visitor's involuntary sadism there. But was my horror about how people there felt, or was it about how their vulnerability made me feel?

My loathing for weakness was a habit that made sense for me as a child; perhaps it allowed me to function, to get on with my life. But as I reached and then passed forty and neared forty-five, I wondered if I'd gotten on with life by avoiding a lot of it. It's been a few years since I've been in love, longer since I've thought I might marry. Seeing how the Afghans meet life head-on is making me suspect that real vulnerability, the kind whose dosage you can't control, is worth experiencing.

The first margarita, the first brownie, the first burrito in a month pall quickly. The thrill of wearing soft, clean, comfortable clothes all the time soon fades. I feel depressed by what looks like the triviality of my life and my culture. What justifies my return? I tell myself that it's my friends, my work, and the possibilities for change and astonishment that New York offers, but I'm not convinced.

I think a lot about my three weeks with Nabila and Abdul Hasib's family in Mazar and Maimana. The life of my great grandparents in the Baltic States probably was similar. Substitute the routines of Judaism for those of Sunni Islam, and my ancestors would have felt at home. It was this traditional world that my parents, and most second-generation American Jews, had been so eager to banish from their lives. I rejected the Jewish part of my own upbringing, and I wasn't about to embrace Islam, but I felt at home in Mazar more than I ever had in my parents' suburban New Jersey house.

If I'd been told at twenty that I'd ever feel this way, I wouldn't

have believed it. In 1978 I didn't want to go to Herat to learn
how to live, just to see the monuments and general exoticism.
I loved Islamic architecture, but I thought contemporary Islamic society was backward. I concentrated in ancient Greek
philosophy at Harvard because I believed in the free movement of thought and argument, which were values opposed
to those of traditional societies and religion.

My Jewishness was valuable to me only as far as it was com-
patible with being an intellectual. Like many American Jews,
I'd grown up thinking that Jews were among the standard-
bearers of the high culture of Europe. That my impoverished
great-grandparents attended the opera when they immigrated
to New York was somehow connected with their Jewishness.

But after my second trip to Afghanistan I'm less sure that my
heritage is the opera and what it represents. The kings in
Jerusalem, from whose names my mother's father's family
claimed distinction, were in truth ragged warlords, savage,
polygamous, and autocratic, with next to nothing in common
with the world of Verdi and Mozart. King David—who mur-
dered a man so he could marry his wife—made most Afghan
warlords look good.

After 9/11, I'd been as eager as anyone to defend the United
States and what are loosely called Western values against terror-
ists and unreason. But my trips to Afghanistan haven't re-
inforced this simple picture. It now seems to me that when we
defend the tradition of free inquiry, for which Socrates died,
against the dead hand of custom, we oppose one East to another.

Plato's Athens was an Eastern city. The seclusion, veiling,

and—to be frank—oppression of Athenian women was not a bizarre contradiction to Athenian democracy and to the free movement of thought in the dialogues of Plato. It was not as though democracy and the dialectic were "ours" and the harem was something else, some accidental element that would eventually drop by the wayside. They fit into a unified whole as much as the rough egalitarianism of the Arab tribes meshed with the religion of Mohammed. Plato was as Middle Eastern as Moses or Mohammed in many ways: in his underlying assumption of a face-to-face community of more or less equal male citizens defined by their worship of common gods; in his search for moral certainties that could be used to persuade men to behave well; in his suspicion of art and image making shared by Judaism and Islam as well. And even Plato's willingness to use rhetoric and the euphony of language, as much as argument and logic, to persuade others of his beliefs calls the Quran to mind.

We like to place on one side civil society, public institutions, the legal and social equality of men and women, and the right to pursue reason where it leads. And on the other side are tribal or clan society, the embrace of the extended family, patriarchy, and the dominance of tradition. But just as masculinity and femininity are not polarities but complementary concepts that don't make sense without each other, so West and East are a pair that exists in dynamic tension.

And then there is the matter of my heart. I'm no longer eager to identify with what I used to think of as the West. While I'm more patriotic than I've ever been and while I support American policies in Afghanistan, I no longer believe I owe my intellectual and emotional allegiances solely to the cultures of

Europe and America. I've fallen in love—albeit an ambivalent and critical love—with the traditional Islamic world most Americans think threatens us. I found in Mazar not only hospitality but kindness and tenderness that are in short supply in my life in the United States and in my travels in the rich democracies. I felt more at home in Afghanistan than I had in Israel, and more loved.

At the same time, much of what I saw in Afghanistan disturbed me. Apart from the poverty and lack of education and the fraught issue of women's rights, Afghan society has its moral fault lines. The best epigram I've ever seen about Afghans explains the problem. It comes from the first Afghan American novel, *The Kite Runner,* by the talented San Francisco physician Khaled Hosseini: "Afghans cherish customs but abhor rules."

Hosseini's epigram can be unpacked to explain what I came to see, by the end of my second trip, as the Afghans' tragic national flaw: risk aversion. Decisions aren't made except by default. No one will take responsibility, lest action end in defeat, which lowers status. Especially for those born into higher-status families, there's more to be lost by trying and failing than there is to be gained by trying and succeeding.

Coasting on the familiar tide of custom, insulated from the need for organized institutions by their network of cousins, Afghans have been motivated to develop only the merest skeleton of a civil society. Afghans don't have friends, they have cousins. As Charles Lindholm points out in his study of the Pashtun, the friend can be neither of higher status nor of lower, and if he is equal he is a rival. Only the foreigner or stranger is an unthreatening friend; extravagant traditions of hospitality to strangers have grown up around that idea. I was the beneficiary of some of this customary goodwill in Mazar and Maimana.

The Afghan propensity for risk aversion, rather than a propensity for violence, may be the best explanation for Afghanistan's often-decried "warlordism": When thinking big is outlawed, only outlaws will think big. Most "warlords" in Afghan society are strivers from poorly connected, low-status families. General Dostum fits the bill. Like many strivers in the United States and Europe a generation or two ago, he found in the army a means of escaping the poverty of his peasant origins. He didn't have the option open to members of Afghanistan's *khan* class—the landed gentry, the class Abdul Hasib's and Najib's and Amir's families belong to—of collecting advanced degrees and impressive job titles while living off his landholdings.

Precisely because few people want to rock the boat, it's easily tipped over when someone does. Bad geopolitical luck, combined with the lack of strong civil institutions, leaves custom and the gun as the two easy alternatives. Afghans can't seem to stop killing each other because, like a couple in a bad marriage, they've never tried the scary venture of learning to have survivable fights. There is little room in the society for passionate discussion without physical consequences. Newspaper editorialists who go too far in advocating secularism still find themselves fleeing for their lives. Just before the October 2004 presidential elections, the Supreme Court of Afghanistan tried to disqualify one of the candidates, Abdul Latif Pedram, a noted poet living in exile in France, for the blasphemous act of opposing polygamy.

We Americans, on the other hand, follow rules. We don't leave much to the realm of tradition, and our traditions are unmanageably diverse anyhow. We interrogate and debate everything. We are never satisfied. While we have created an immensely rich culture and a civil society that makes good on many of the utopian promises of five thousand years of dreamers— Religious freedom! Legal equality of the sexes! Universal free education!—all too often we have the taste of ashes in our mouths.

The opposition isn't just between Afghan and American ways, but between the traditional and developed worlds. One day I quoted Hosseini's epigram to my friend Samuel, and because he was from a developing country, Colombia, he knew immediately what I meant.

"You think people are nicer in places like Afghanistan, and I agree with you. They are nicer in Colombia, too. But we are nicer because we have no rules. We have customs because we have no rules—you can put it that way. That is how we get things done. It is not just Afghanistan or Colombia. All Third World countries are like that."

I felt a great relief at Samuel's words. Now I understood my long love affair with the Third World. If the American ability to get things done could be united with the Afghan warmth in doing them, we might have a society I'd enjoy living in. As it is, I find New York cold in comparison to Afghanistan, people's preoccupations unfathomable. I've never been interested in consumerism and television and fast food, the debate over which conditioner to use or which restaurant has the best *mojito*. I don't want to move to Mazar, much less to Maimana, and live in a family compound, but I'm finding that I don't want to go on as I have before.

part two

It is always dark inside the heart
because it is inside the body.

—Fragment of the poetry of
Yehuda Amichai

I lean toward the fireplace, my face warmed as my back is chilled by a draft from the front door. My sweater is too short to keep out the late-January cold, but it's one I felt Amir would like: not obviously sexy, but offering more of a look at my figure than I've shown him alone before. And now I offer him another glass of red wine, emptying the bottle.

A week ago he'd offered me a Dari lesson, to teach me the Afghan words Shirin didn't know, he'd claimed, but I thought I heard an insinuation even over the phone. I flirted right back, for once, and arranged tonight's meeting. And my notebook has long since been closed. It's eleven, and Amir is telling me about his romantic history. A couple of months ago he broke up for the final time with the love of his life, his college girlfriend. They'd been talking about getting back together, although she lives in Seattle with her boyfriend. But something had gone wrong.

The only woman I've ever loved, he repeats, and I try to look fascinated. He doesn't know that I've already heard the whole thing from Shirin. You might not even remember her name by the time you're my age, I snap. I'm jealous, I realize with alarm, and remind myself that Amir is used to women much younger than I and wants to marry a teenager. I have to force myself to think realistically.

The fire is dying down. Amir watches as I prod the logs with the poker, trying to show him how firm my arms are. He seems to realize a change of topic is called for and begins, At Princeton I studied French. They told me I had a good accent—Farsi uses some of the same sounds as French.

Then he pauses and looks straight at me, smiling, and says very softly, *Voulez-vous coucher avec moi ce soir?*

I smile back, remembering the disco hit of my college days. It surprises me that he knows it; Amir would have been a kid when that song was popular. The tune was catchy, but I'd sneered at the lyrics. No one would use *vous,* the formal form of "you," to proposition a woman.

Amir repeats his question, but I'm paralyzed. Perhaps it's the tenderness in his voice that makes me doubt whether he really means what he says. I've grown used to associating sex with lust, and I don't see any in his eyes or voice.

You have beautiful hands, I say. I'd never noticed before, but they are so perfect I want to hide my own, with their veins raised by age.

Thank you, he says, still looking me in the eye, and I throw another log on the fire.

Just then Amir's cell phone rings and he takes the call, suddenly matter-of-fact. "Yes, I'll be there in fifteen minutes," he says, and hangs up.

I've arranged to go to meet my friend Ellen, he explains. She needs my advice on a date she just had. She's my best woman friend.

I bite my lip; just a little while ago he said he'd stay until I kicked him out. But maybe I ruined things when I didn't respond to his French question. I make an effort at a smile and turn my attention to the fire so Amir won't see my disappointment. Then I say, Well, I'll be seeing you tomorrow anyway. I've invited plenty of tall women to counterbalance me and Shirin.

A week ago Amir also suggested that he and Shirin and I cook some Afghan food at my house for a small dinner. It sounded promising. We set the date, January 31. But then he asked, Can you invite some tall, hot women? I concealed my disappointment. Then I got on the phone and in a spirit of revenge, invited the tallest people I knew, including my Colombian friends Samuel and his wife, Rebecca, six-three and five-ten respectively, and another woman of Rebecca's height.

Now Amir seems to sense my hurt. He protests, all sweetness: But I consider you tall.

Me? I'm five-six on a windy day. But that's kind of you.

You're a good height.

Why don't you have Ellen meet you here?

She is a small, sweet, unconfident girl, not at all what I imagined. Somehow the talk goes from Ellen's date to my opinion of men. I try not to sound harsh.

You're in love with your father, Amir says suddenly to me, aren't you?

I'm not too keen on American men these days.

Am I included?

No, you're an Afghan. If I had a younger sister I'd recommend you to her with only one reservation.

What's that?

But as I'm about to answer, my phone rings and I deliberately take the call. By the time I finish, I've forgotten what my reservation was, and Ellen and Amir leave for their tête-à-tête. That night I can't sleep; I can't think about anything but Amir.

In hindsight, I wasn't thinking much at all. I suspected that half the attraction of Amir's college girlfriend was that she was safely remote and unavailable. But it never occurred to me to talk with Amir about his views of love or dating or how they fit with his plan for an arranged marriage. What had his romantic life been like? I had no idea. How did he treat the women he dated? I'd never even asked him about what had happened between him and Shirin in the fall.

A few days after I returned from Afghanistan in early December, I'd invited Shirin and Amir over for dinner. The evening felt a little stiff, but I put that down to my disappointment at being back in New York. I couldn't remember quite why I had been looking forward to seeing Amir, and he didn't seem to understand my feelings about my trip. Shirin did, since she went back to Iran many summers to see her family. And after Amir left, she admitted that she hadn't felt comfortable with him around.

"I haven't seen Amir in a couple of weeks. Amir wasn't very nice after the last night we spent together. He came over to my apartment, and I made Iranian food for him and we read Hafez together. He really knows poetry, much more than I do. I had a better time than the first night, and I was starting to kind of like him. But after that he never called.

"We were more just friends anyway—he invited me to a lot of parties; we didn't spend much time by ourselves. It wasn't a romantic thing for either one of us. I think he was upset because this old girfriend of his decided not to see him. But I don't know how serious that was—I mean he slept with me anyway, even though he was supposed to be in love with her.

"He has issues with women. He told me he doesn't talk to his younger brother because he married a woman from Iran. He said it would be a problem if he wanted to marry me, because I'm from Iran, and I'm a few months older than he is. He thinks no one is as good as an Afghan."

I didn't pay much attention to what Shirin said; it looked as if she'd be getting back together with her ex, George. I didn't register how insulted I would have felt if a man told me he didn't talk to his younger brother because he married a Jewish woman. But when I came back from my trip, I was less intrigued by Amir than when I'd left. The e-mail he sent me in Afghanistan didn't interest me much; I couldn't even remember what he wrote. When he suggested that the two of us get together a few days before Christmas, being alone with him never occurred to me. Instead, I took him to my friend Maud's house to meet her father and sisters, who were visiting for the holidays. Everyone loved him, and he seemed at home although he was the youngest person there.

Maud, observant and outspoken, took me aside and asked why I wasn't interested in Amir. Was he single? I explained that he was intent on marrying an Afghan virgin. She laughed.

"Well, you don't have to marry him. Why don't you just date him?"

"Too young."

By Christmas Day my feelings had changed. Maud was having a party, and I told Shirin and Amir they had to come so I wouldn't be the only non-Christian there. But only Shirin showed up. Amir, when Shirin finally called him, said he was too hungover to come out. That was a surprise. I'd never seen him drink to the point of being visibly drunk, but when she got off the phone Shirin told me he'd even had a beer at a party they went to during Ramazan. That made him seem less foreign, if more hypocritical. I was relieved, because I had given him a copy of my memoir of my heroin years and I had feared his disapproval.

Maud sensed my disappointment as Shirin reported her conversation, and asked again, "Are you sure he's not for you?"

I mentioned our age difference once more. "And he reads the Quran all the time." But as I spoke I finally admitted to myself that I was attracted to Amir. The problem was that I was pretty sure he wasn't attracted to me. When Amir called a day later, he said he wasn't sure he'd be able to make it to my New Year's party because he'd be with a group of Princeton friends.

I'm not feeling too great, anyway, he added. Maybe we should just see each other in January. I was disappointed but I told him to come by if he felt like it. Much to my surprise, he did. I wasn't thrilled with the friends he had in tow, a supercilious bunch of preppies, but I was so happy to see Amir that I had to keep myself from hovering around him.

A month later, and the night after Amir's Dari lesson, I finally get what I had hardly admitted longing for on New Year's. At three in the morning, when Shirin and the tall people have finally left, Amir and I are alone. I take off my shoes and curl my legs up around myself on the couch. Amir is still sitting across the room on an uncomfortable chair and I motion to him to join me. He sits down very close to me but also on top of my legs, and I almost laugh. He must be pretty drunk, as I am. We began the evening with champagne, drank wine with dinner, and are now making our way through a fifth of bourbon.

Still crushing my leg, Amir leans over and kisses me. Sweet, even innocent, is my first reaction, and then I'm overwhelmed. Within a few minutes I know I was right to want this. I'd feared Amir wouldn't be good in bed, but that phrase seems irrelevant to what's happening.

Amir asks, Would you like another drink?

I can only say hoarsely, Why not?

Later, he wonders if I have any Barry White. I know a woman who says it's the best music for making love.

I haven't heard a man talk about *making love* in a long time. A moment after the impulse to poke fun at Amir passes, I'm moved. I overlook his clumsily disguised reference to a former girlfriend, and his tacky taste in music. By now I'm finding everything about him endearing—even stuff I normally have no tolerance for, like his finishing most of the bottle of bourbon by himself. I can't get enough of his smell, his skin, his kisses.

Shall we go upstairs? he asks.

Why not? I say again. And Amir lifts me in his arms and carries me to the base of the stairs. Then, wisdom overcoming his romantic impulse, he puts me down; it's three flights to my bedroom.

We never go to sleep. We can't keep apart. I can hardly talk, but Amir, usually laconic, rambles on in his low, melodic, and nearly unaccented English, calling me *honey,* confessing, It's been years since I've felt like this. And then, words that leap out when I'm not really paying attention: That's why I love you so much.

I'm dazed.

This isn't my usual way. I'm very careful to distinguish between love, which blindsides me every half decade or so, and sex, which I enjoy especially with strangers. Usually sex is a thrill--taking off my clothes the first time, learning a man's body, being surprised by what is particular to him in bed—a thrill along the lines of going to a good new restaurant. What happens with Amir is something else. It's more like landing in a country I've never been to before.

I speculate on what it would be like to live with Amir and force myself to remember that when he's forty, I'll be fifty. What will he think of my looks then? And then I tell myself that this romance is doomed even before I become old and ugly. Amir keeps telling me that he's going back to Afghanistan very soon, probably by Norouz, the Persian New Year, March 21. He'll stay for six months or more and look for a bride among his cousins.

It's not enough to have an arranged marriage with a virgin; it turns out that only a cousin will do. Amir's parents, he admits, are first cousins; I suspect he has only told me because I mentioned that Nabila and Abdul Hasib are first cousins. Amir knows enough to realize that most Americans find this sort of thing primitive. But he also tells me without embarrassment that his parents have tried to interest him in a first cousin once removed in San Francisco. To my relief, he says she isn't cute or especially young, and they've never met. But I don't understand his reasoning. What's the point of marrying a relative when there's no longer any property to keep in the family?

It's tradition, he explains. All of us have married relatives, except one of my brothers. My lost brother. I don't talk to him.

So it doesn't matter that Amir looks like someone in my family, it doesn't matter that he says my brother is handsome by Afghan standards, and it doesn't matter that he says a lot of Afghan women are too dark for him, but I'm just right. I am not an Afghan, much less a cousin.

At the moment, this doesn't seem to be inhibiting Amir.

So will you come to meet me in Dubai when I'm in Afghanistan? he asks. I'm going to leave you all my books when I go overseas. Maybe we can go to Florida together before I leave. Ellen and my friend Don and I have talked about going to see a friend who owns a restaurant in South Beach. We can party.

The enthusiasm in Amir's voice as he talks about partying reminds me that he's ten years younger than me. At his age I would have talked the same way, but now I can't think of many things I'd less enjoy on a vacation than hanging out in clubs and bars. I weigh this against how I feel now as he curls his feet around mine.

Turn the clock to the wall, Amir had commanded when we got into my bed after hours entwined on my living-room couch. When I look at the clock again it's afternoon, and we've made love twelve times, a lifetime record for both of us. I haven't slept and neither has Amir.

I make him coffee, which he likes very strong and sweet. I drink ten cups of coffee a day at work, he tells me.

No wonder you don't sleep!

I have problems with that, he admits, though it's better than it used to be.

There goes my theory that Afghans don't have insomnia.

It would be better if you cut down on the coffee, I suggest. I'm relieved that he doesn't ask me what my problem is, because I don't know. I've noticed that I can fall asleep even on the first night with a new man if all I feel for him is lust.

By the time Amir leaves at dusk, I'm in love.

9 | *a love letter*

Two nights later, Amir cries in front of me.

Amir and my tall Colombian friend Rebecca have invited me to the same small party at a bar. By coincidence, Rebecca is curating a photography exhibit with Amir's best friend, Don, and it's the birthday of one of the artists. Rebecca and Luisa and Jason come over to my house to wait for Amir to arrive.

When Amir walks in from the January cold, I'm filled with emotion. Everything about him feels perfect to me, even his hooked nose and short arms and bad tan shoes. I've just been on the phone with Maud admitting that Amir is for me after all. It's going to be difficult, but I can't imagine giving up what I discovered two nights ago. Just as Amir knocks on the door, Rebecca is telling me that she approves. "I could tell from the way you looked next to each other at the dinner two nights ago. You're texturally correct for each other." When Luisa asks what "texturally correct" means, Rebecca explains, "You know, the smell, the skin, everything is right." She's a keen observer, Rebecca, and her foreigner's English neologisms often get at truths I haven't seen. I remember that Shirin said Amir had a good smell. Maybe it all came down to that.

But as soon as Amir comes in, something is wrong. Amir is cold from the start. He kisses me on the cheek hastily and keeps a distance. As everyone leaves my house to hail a cab, Amir walks ahead with the others as I lock the door. I feel terrible.

At the bar he relaxes a little and gets me a drink. I whisper in his ear, You make me hot.

That's a bad thing. You should have self-control.

I look for a sign that Amir is kidding, but there's venom in his voice. I almost walk out then and there. *No,* I tell myself, *don't do that. Anger comes so easily to you. Try to figure out what's going on.*

Then Amir says, I'd like to fuck Luisa.

I'm afraid Jason has heard. Luisa's been seeing him since they met at my dinner three months ago. I know Amir's trying to enrage me, because despite her beauty, he didn't seem to notice Luisa when they met that night. Nor is he responding to any signals from her. Like Shirin and Dina and most of my other women friends from the Third World, she favors tall, blond WASPs. Luisa has mixed feelings about Amir anyway. Her comment overall is, "Another Third World aristocrat who needs to get over himself." When I told her yesterday about his request for Barry White, she said, "All Third World boys like Barry White."

Amir shouldn't have another drink, not one—he's already unsteady on his feet—but he buys tequila shots for himself and me and a friend. The tab is seventy-five dollars after fifteen minutes, and he throws his credit card down on the bar. I say something about the cost and he says, slurring his words, Alcohol is the only thing I spend money on.

This is a new side of Amir, hinted at in his Christmas Day hangover. In the fall he'd never had more than a glass of wine or so in my presence, and while we'd both had a lot of liquor our first night as lovers, I put that down to nerves. But maybe he drinks more than I'd realized.

My relationship with alcohol is peculiar. After a couple of drinks, liquor acts like speed with me: I stay up all night. It seems unfair, since I've never been a heavy drinker, but I snorted heroin for years. My body learned to metabolize central nervous system depressants all too well. So I rarely have more than a drink or two—there's no point in it. And I don't like being around people who are obviously drunk, and still less so when their drinking feels compulsive, as Amir's does tonight. It isn't about pleasure at all.

Amir sits down next to me and his friends and swallows another shot, his handsome face flushed with alcohol. Should I leave? He's making me unbearably sad. All of the promise of last night has dissolved. I'm back to what I've grown used to thinking of as the grimness of my real life.

One of Amir's friends comes up to me and says, "Hi, I'm Bill. I hear you're a famous journalist."

Since I'm neither famous nor a journalist, Amir must have

bragged about me to his friend. That's sweet. I'm so touched that I forget how much I hate being called a journalist. But then, an engineer like Amir couldn't be expected to be sensitive to the nuances of writer versus journalist. I talk for a while with Bill as Amir chats with Luisa just out of earshot.

I get up to go to the bathroom, determined to turn the dynamic between me and Amir around. A day later, Luisa tells me, "As soon as you got up he couldn't concentrate on our conversation at all. Every fifteen seconds his eyes went to the bathroom door." She sounded surprised; Luisa's not used to men taking their eyes elsewhere. And in retrospect I am moved. But that night I haven't seen his eyes. And when I return I pull him aside and whisper, I don't like the way you're treating me.

Looking at me coldly he says, Scale down your expectations. I can't be your boyfriend; I'm leaving the country soon.

This makes me feel sick. My expectations of men are already very low, but I still thought that a man who held me in his arms all night two days ago might refrain from telling me he wants to fuck my friends. I think again about leaving. But then Amir puts his arm around me and holds me to his chest; I reach up and kiss him on the neck and I feel the most overwhelming sweetness. Touching his skin is pure joy. We hold hands for a moment, and I feel he loves me, no matter what he just said. Then he downs another shot of tequila.

Rebecca and Luisa and Jason and Amir's friends see which way things are going, make their excuses, and leave. The bar is closing anyway.

I'm going home, Amir.

Okay, I'll be there soon, I just need a little time. His speech is slurred, but his voice is amiable again, his eyes soft. I walk out, but then I look back and see him through the window, struggling to put on his heavy gray wool overcoat. He can't even put his arm through the sleeve. I'd never leave a friend that drunk by himself, so I return.

Why did you come back?

I wanted a cigarette, I say, so as not to shame him, and Amir laughs. We're on the same side again. He hands me one and just manages to light it for me. I help him on with his coat and we get a cab to my house.

He's so drunk he can't walk up the three flights of stairs to my bedroom. He tells me he'll sleep on the sofa where we first made love. I go upstairs, but even there I can hear him moaning in his sleep, although I can't understand what he's saying. I can't sleep. I come downstairs and lie next to him and hold him, and somehow, so drunk, he starts to do what I want.

Wait, we need something, he says, and staggers across the room to his jacket to get a condom.

How did you remember that when you're drunk?

It's the Afghan part of my brain, honey.

And then I remember that he fought in a guerrilla war and must have learned to operate on instinct in ways I've never had to. So it seems natural to ask him what it was like to fight the Soviets.

When we touched on the subject before, Amir said war was exciting. What he says now isn't what I expect.

I fought because we had to. I went with my older brothers and cousins. I can't imagine what it is like for those who committed atrocities, which I did not. For the first years at Princeton I would wake up screaming at night. I had a lot of nightmares. I still don't sleep well, as you know.

He makes a face. And as he describes how his young cousin and comrade in arms was killed in battle fifteen years ago, something in Amir breaks. He's blinking back tears but a few escape, and his body gives up its tension and its pride.

Then he changes the subject as abruptly as I did. He tells me that what he'd said in the bar is true, he can't be my boyfriend. He will only promise that he'll always treat me with respect and that he won't fuck my friends. But that, he says, is all.

I don't think about why he might be saying this just now, and what relation it might or might not have to his tears and the war and my asking about it. I don't make the connection between Amir's groaning in his drunken sleep an hour ago and what he said about his nightmares in college. It only occurs to me much later that his tears must have been as much for himself as for his cousin and that he might have felt my attitude toward war was callous and superficial.

It might have been both of those things, but it wasn't hypocritical. Unlike most women, I've always been fascinated by war. My father had a Bronze Star from his stint in Patton's army, and his war stories had excited me as a child. Later I sought out violence in the proxy forms of martial arts and the drug trade and travel to unstable countries. I was too much a child of the Vietnam era to want to join the army, but I wondered how I would have measured up if women were allowed to face combat.

I should hold Amir and comfort him but I don't—I'm too angry. All I can hear is *that's all,* which shoots straight through my heart.

I find myself shouting at him. How presumptuous! How dare you think I would want you for a boyfriend? Who said I wanted a child for a boyfriend? Do you have any idea how you look to other people when you get drunk like that? You embarrassed me in front of my friends. What makes you think any of them would *want* to fuck you?

Then comes my coup de grâce. And how can you call yourself a Muslim? Doesn't Islam mean submission? What humility do you show before God?

I'm leaving, he says, and he does, a terrible end to our second night together.

I turn off the phone ringer and try to sleep. When I come back downstairs still exhausted a few hours later—no sleep—I send him an e-mail apologizing for losing my temper: *Our feelings for each other are doomed, but I hope we can be together until you leave. Wild horses couldn't drag me away.*

I also write something meant for myself as much as for Amir: *Don't worry about your trip. One goes to Afghanistan under the sign of death, but returns under the sign of life.*

Then I think to check the answering machine and hear Amir's voice, gentle and kind. *I'm sorry that I had to leave and hope you were able to get to sleep, and I hope you have a good day. I'll talk to you soon.* My heart breaks at his simplicity and goodwill and I call him. He hasn't been able to sleep, either. His voice is unsteady now, and hoarse with emotion. He cares about me, I realize, and when he tries to apologize, I won't let him—I don't want to hurt his pride any more than I have already. And I realize that I've hectored him and criticized him while he's never said a word against me.

I sent you an e-mail, I say.

He asks eagerly, A love letter?

What a thought. Who writes love letters anymore?

A nice e-mail, I reply, making my voice stern, hating the banal words. Don't worry.

I know the conventional wisdom is not to see a man who tells me he can't be my boyfriend, much less a man who says the only thing he spends money on is alcohol—much less a man who whispers, *I want to fuck your friend,* when I clearly adore him, and probably because I adore him. But his question suggests that he cares a lot more than he's willing to say.

Amir doesn't know how to be close to a woman for more than

a night, or doesn't want to be. He's from a culture of arranged marriages with no model for dating. He claims he doesn't believe in romantic love, or he's trying to convince himself that he doesn't. And he doesn't know how to reveal himself to me other than all at once or not at all—vileness and sweetness and grief jumbled together, the things you normally disclose in the course of months bursting out in a night or two, like tears. He does know this isn't proper American behavior, but because he acts from a mixture of arrogance and helplessness (qualities often found together), he doesn't care.

I don't care, either. I'm sick of the way I've lived in the last few years and sick of the feeling that my life has already ended. I'll take Amir's real emotion, in all its ambivalence, over the guarded, cagey maneuvers of the New York men I've dated. Amir is a hundred times more alive than they are, and if he's already hurt me badly, our second night together, he has also shown me more of himself. Or so I am thinking—I'm faintly aware that this might be a rationalization, and that it's as simple as this: I can't bear not to see him again.

Khanum Ann! Khub astee? Amir is at the door, his arms full of groceries. It's the night after our fight; he's going to show me how to make one of the dishes he remembers from his childhood.

In the fall, Amir called me *Ann jan,* as Shirin still does. *Khanum* is what I was called by Nabila's family, but it's also the more respectful of the two common Farsi words for wife. A man can refer to his *zan,* his woman, or to his *khanum,* his lady, and the two have the flavor they would have had in eighteenth-century England. And as in that era, *khanum* is used with the first name; the last name is thought too cold. I'm starting to catch on that Amir is all about mixed emotions, and this is typical. Walking in with the groceries like an Afghan husband, he greets me like a wife—or like a foreign stranger.

Here, I brought you something. I won't be needing it soon, because I'll be there! Amir unrolls a large, detailed map of Afghanistan, a newly published one I've read about. I love the gesture, but I'm hurt by his happy anticipation of his trip. Won't he miss me at all?

In the kitchen he hands me a sheaf of recipes downloaded from the Internet, and I'm touched by how much he cares about this dinner. He says Afghan food is the best in the world. I gently tell him that when he gets his green card and can travel to Europe, he might discover otherwise. But I agree that what I had in Mazar and Maimana was delicious. And by chance, Amir grew up on the same dishes I'd sampled, because his family's cook had been Uzbek.

Tonight we're going to make the rice pilaf with lamb chunks called *qabuli pilau,* which Amir tells me means "worthy pilaf." Typical of Afghan food, it's a labor-intensive dish. We're shy and correct with each other as we chop and mix, tentative after our fight, and I'm filled with tenderness for him. Making food with Amir is relaxing, which isn't how I usually feel when cooking with a boyfriend.

I've cooked with other men, of course, though not so many as I probably would have if I'd lived somewhere other than Manhattan, with its thousands of restaurants and food available for delivery almost twenty-four hours a day. With most of the other men, it was more stressful than fun. I had the idea they were trying to show me they could be sensitive men—or worse, that they could do a woman's work better because they were men. Not that they usually can. There is always just the one dish they know, the roast chicken with three kinds of mushrooms or the risotto with shrimp. They've never learned to improvise. And there's an aggressiveness to their preparation of this one dish that dissolves the association of food with nourishment and love. They literally make a mean omelet.

Amir is different. He's naturally gifted in the kitchen—his

knife technique, self-taught, is better than mine after a class—
so there's nothing strenuous about what he does. While he's
unsophisticated about ingredients and teases me for buying
organic meat, he cares about how food tastes, and he knows
how to make delicious dishes. That's something not every
technically accomplished cook can do. Unlike so many men
I've known, Amir cooks not to prove a point but to give us
both pleasure.

And yet, he is proving a point. Amir has told me what I already
knew, that Afghan men do not cook unless there are no
women around, as in war, or unless they are servants. Cooks
in rich houses are usually men, often poor relatives; unrelated
women would never work in an Afghan house. Amir's mother
shared the cooking with a servant, but Amir would have been
laughed at had he said he wanted to learn. "A wife is for the
kitchen," as he told Luisa. So he's pieced together his knowledge from aunts, cousins, the Internet, and memory. When he
goes back, he tells me, he'll be able to eat his fill of many delicious dishes but not cook them himself. So this exercise in
nostalgia and tradition is—like so much about Amir—also a
defiance of the culture he idolizes.

Amir teaches me how to make the dishes he misses, buys me
supplies he thinks I need, cajoles me into getting a spice rack,
and finally suggests a rice cooker—at which I draw the line in
Afghanization. We're playing house, and it must mean more
to him, for he hasn't had a home in decades.

Amir refuses to let me visit his place in Brooklyn Heights, ob-
jecting mildly, It's not so great, you know. When I ask why
Shirin has seen it, he says he didn't intend it: But, you know,

she lives in Brooklyn, too, and she called when she happened to be in the neighborhood—I couldn't say no. Shirin says this refusal is one of Amir's few smart moves with me. "His place is filthy. You wouldn't like it. The bathroom is disgusting."

I don't press him; I have my own issues with domesticity. I bought my first house at twenty-seven, I've given big dinner parties since I was just out of school, but even the word *home* makes me anxious. I don't have many good memories of my childhood, and these few tend to be about vacations, not about our home life. When I went away to camp at the age of nine, I was never homesick. My memories of home evoke isolation, loneliness, anxiety. Perhaps these states felt natural to my parents and have come to seem natural to me and my brother. My father has been dead for twenty-some years, and my mother, brother, and I have all lived alone for at least that long. This was not easy for the family I lived with in Mazar to understand. It might have been what they found most baffling about me—even more than my being unmarried and childless. That trip made it harder for me to understand, too.

Since Scott, I've never lived with a man. Once I came close to moving in with someone, but that was almost fifteen years ago. I haven't wanted to live with most of the men I've dated since. I haven't even wanted to hang out at home with them. Those romances had been centered on going out rather than staying in, especially during my rock and drug years, when I half lived in clubs and bars. Sex was the only reason to go home.

Now for the first time in a long while, I see a way to enjoy domestic life. It doesn't seem stifling and claustrophobic the way it has for many years. I don't feel in danger of turning into my mother, because my time with Amir is pure pleasure. We hardly bother to put on clothes, or not for long. Food cools while we go upstairs and then back downstairs to eat it, wearing even fewer clothes. Courses are separated by long intermissions. Sometimes we make love in the kitchen that Amir says a wife is for. Keeping house flows naturally out of making love, I suddenly feel; having a home is part of expressing your affection for someone. Much of the rest of the world seems to have understood this all along, but I'm discovering it in my forties.

I'm also learning that when I'm with a man, we don't have to talk all the time. Amir and I do talk, but it's not so much about anything in particular as for the pleasure of being with each other—stray remarks about Afghanistan, our childhoods, our college days. Maybe I'm able to enjoy this as a result of my stay in Nabila and Abdul Hasib's compound. People who spend time with the same cousins day after day and night after night don't always have much new to say to one another. Communicating information and opinions isn't what they do when they talk; they mainly express their feelings for each other, or their place in the family structure.

I didn't have a good sense of this because in my family we always talked about subjects: the election, civil rights, my dad's war stories, what he did at work that day. Conversation had to go somewhere, teach something, reach a conclusion. But something in me has changed since coming back, I'm realizing. Now I'm able to be silent more often. I think of a quote from a British writer, Edward St. Aubyn, which calls the soul the part of the mind "not dominated by the need to talk."

When the *qabuli pilau* is ready, Amir shows me how to eat with my hands, as Afghans do. It's difficult to scoop up the rice and lamb pieces gracefully, and I feel uncouth. It's not only the first time I've tried, it's the first time it hasn't made me queasy to watch. In Nabila's house, I avoided learning to eat with my hands. It was a final barrier I was unable to cross. I even had trouble taking a portion from a platter someone had just put his or her hand into. But now it feels fine.

The bad Amir of the other night seems far away. We've only had a glass of wine each and he's gentle and reasonable, the way he was in the fall, before we became lovers. Just before we go up to bed for the night he asks, Can we have a little more wine? This is less than the recommendation of the surgeon general for avoiding heart disease!

We've talked a little about his drinking. In my e-mail of the day before, I asked, *How about if sometimes when we see each other, we don't drink?* And he replied, *I like* sh'rub (the Farsi for wine) *and drink a lot when I can, but I have also gone days and weeks without drinking.*

I know that this is meant to comfort me, but it reminds me of years gone by when I used to count the days since I'd last snorted dope.

Then we have that second glass of wine each, and he's still lovely, and then we're in bed and a condom breaks. He's worried.

I wouldn't mind if I got pregnant, I tease, realizing that with him I'd be thrilled to. It feels right that I'd get pregnant given that we spend so much of our time together in bed. No, he's not ready to be a father, we probably aren't going to be together when he gets back from Afghanistan, but so what? We could be friends, if not lovers. He seems calm and reasonable enough to weather that inevitable transition. And I'm prepared to be a mother, even a single mother. I have a good income and a town house and a car. By the time our child talks, my Persian should be decent; I can talk to her and Amir can give her lessons. I picture a daughter looking like Loulou and with her charm and intelligence.

A child should be raised in a marriage, Amir replies tensely, talking as though a child were a real possibility. Doesn't he realize how difficult it is for a woman of forty-four to get pregnant, even if she and her partner are trying? I think about asking if that's a proposal, but what I say instead comes out of instinct:

Who are your ancestors? Maybe I've gotten a little ahead of myself in saying I'd have your child. We're descended from King David on my mother's father's side.

Amir understands me, as I knew he would. It's because I've already gathered that his family is an old one that I'm not afraid I'll shame him by asking his ancestry. But I'm surprised when he names an Arab of the seventh century known to every Muslim, one of the most important figures in Islam after Mohammed and Ali. In a Christian context it would be like being descended from Saint Paul.

That will do, I say. So you're a Semite, too.

For years I had only thought of having a child with a Jew, no matter how badly I got along with my Jewish boyfriends. It was a matter of blood. It might be that I can allow myself to escape my own madness with Amir because I can see how he is caught in his.

We make love again and try to sleep for a while, and then Amir says, I have this idea that I will die a violent death if I go back to Afghanistan.

That's the kind I would prefer, I say. If you'd seen your father with Parkinson's disease, you might think there are worse things than a clean shot in the head.

I'm starting to feel that Luisa was right—Amir plays the Afghan card at every opportunity. It doesn't occur to me till much later that it was a huge thing for an Afghan man to admit to being afraid, that it meant Amir was starting to trust me. And I showed him no sympathy.

The next morning as he leaves for work, he kisses me and says in a low voice, I hope nothing is growing down there.

I'd already forgotten. But I blurt out, I hope there is, but it's up to God now, isn't it?

from: sarahfromsavannah@ihug.co.nz.
to: annmarlowe@hotmail.com

Afghan men are delightful to date, so long as you maintain the upper hand and can walk away at any moment. But when push comes to shove, the old double standard raises its head. They marry one of their own. The ones I know have all ultimately behaved like cads to the Western women they've been involved with.
Sarah

This e-mail terrifies me. Sarah isn't a close friend, she's twenty years older than I am, and she doesn't know much about my emotional life. I only mentioned that I'd started dating Amir because I'd e-mailed her briefly about him when he and I were just friends. But I take her warning seriously. She spent a good part of the sixties working in Afghanistan, and she's even more obsessed with the country than I am. Even now that she's living with her retired diplomat husband in Auckland, she e-mails me news items about Afghanistan.

Just a few days after the night when the condom broke, it chills me to realize that Amir's mixture of desire and flight, sweetness and cruelty, might follow a cultural pattern rather than reflect an individual struggle. I hear Amir's opinions on arranged marriage as crazy. But they might be the most sane thing about him, the one instance in which he can hold on to the beliefs of his childhood. And the caution, *so long as you maintain the upper hand and can walk away at any moment,* also gives me a start.

I'd originally thought Amir's bad behavior was out of his control, and that made it easier to take. But what looked like giving in to uncontrollable impulses might be much more calculated, a proven strategy—and not even a personal strategy but an Afghan strategy for keeping women off balance. I remember an earlier boyfriend, a psychiatrist, who behaved as erratically as Amir and proposed to me a year after we'd broken up. One of his friends, also a shrink, advised me, "Bullies are asking for limits."

Former philosophy student that I am, I reflexively come up with objections to Sarah's conclusions. What if I were to substitute the word *Jewish* for *Afghan* and project myself back in time to 1950? Wouldn't it have been true that most of the Jewish men of my father's generation might have happily dated Christian women but ultimately married Jews? Did that make them cads? Were they? Had my father behaved badly to the women he'd dated before my mother? And did Christian Americans then watch him closely for signs of caddish behavior, pushiness, greed? What about their behavior to women? Was he held to a higher standard? If Christians are entitled to date Jewish women and then marry one of their own, isn't Amir?

I can't see things as Amir does, but I can understand by analogy. I know what it's like to be in a tiny minority and to have to worry about how others see you. I remember my family's commemoration of Jewish holidays. We lived in towns where maybe 10 percent or fewer of the residents were Jewish, and that was a lot compared with our 2 percent of the American population. My parents were not observant. We never went to synagogue. But my parents insisted that we stay home from school on the major holidays and, while at home, stay indoors. The point of our absence from school was to show that we were not ashamed of being Jewish (not proud of being Jewish, just not ashamed—I noticed that). And the point of staying indoors was to convince the Christian neighbors that we took our religion seriously. We had a front to maintain, always. Being a Jew, I gradually learned, wasn't so simple.

Amir had experienced something similar in college. He told me how when he first arrived at Princeton, his freshman advisor told him that he had to bear in mind that he'd be the first person from Afghanistan whom most of his classmates had ever met. He had to be sure to give them a good impression, to act as though he were an ambassador of his country. I've always tried to remember that, he said.

But the burden of being the model Afghan boy might have been part of what led him to get drunk sometimes. Most of the time I saw Amir once we started dating, he was drinking.

I can't condemn Amir if he wanted to escape himself. I'd acted on the same desires. When I used heroin for seven years in the late eighties and early nineties, I was oblivious to some of the ways people reacted to me on dope.

But what disturbs me most about Amir's drinking isn't his part in it but mine: I like him better when he's a little drunk. Cold sober, he can be hard, distant, inaccessible. After a few drinks he's a gentler, more affectionate man, a man who murmurs, *You look absolutely beautiful,* and makes me feel well loved. If he gets drunk around me because it allows him to be intimate, I give him credit for the desire for closeness and for his willingness to show himself to me at his most vulnerable.

But Amir's drinking will have a natural end soon, anyway, like our romance, when he goes to Afghanistan in a month or so. Alcohol isn't part of Afghan life, and it's illegal for Afghans to buy, though it's available in the cities where expatriates live. When I ask him once if he'll miss drinking when he's in Afghanistan, he says that, on the contrary, he is looking forward to taking a break from it. So I'm not too worried about him. There is such a short time now to Norouz—Persian New Year.

On a long February night I reach into my closet and show Amir my small collection of traditional clothes from Afghanistan. When I pull out a heavy gold-embroidered maroon velvet gown, he draws in his breath, and says, That's a Pashtun party dress! Can you put it on?

I hesitate. The bulky dress, three sizes too big, isn't flattering. It was a gift from the head of the orphanage I'd helped in Shebergan in May—and I remember how my American friends laughed when I wore it at dinner to honor the woman who gave it to me. But Amir's excitement makes me put it on. I'm incredulous when he admires it.

Can I touch the knickers? My jaw drops. He thinks he needs permission to touch my knickers? They're hideous, besides, baggy grass-green harem pants of cheap polyester. Amir pleads, I never got to do that.

Then I get it. His mother hadn't worn stockings or heels; like the family I'd lived among, she would have gone barefoot in their compound. But like all Afghan women she would have worn pants underneath her skirt or dress. The knickers are for him the fetish object that garters and heels might be for a man whose mother had worn them in the 1950s.

Amir pulls me into bed again, aroused by the garish knickers.

Later I ask him something I've been curious about since my dinner party in October: Have you ever actually had sex with a virgin? Yes, once in college. It was horrible.

I try not to show him my relief.

Toward dawn, we investigate the erotic possibilities of the other traditional Afghan garment I own, the *chad'ri*. This is the garment incorrectly known in the West as the burka (Arabic for "curtain"). Just about the first question I'm asked when I mention my trips to Afghanistan is whether I had to wear one. And I reply that I wore not a *chad'ri* but a chador, or head scarf. Traditionally all Shiite and most Sunni interpreters of the Quran have held that its few and mysterious remarks on veiling allow a woman's face, hands, and feet to be seen. It's only the most extreme Sunnis who believe in covering women's faces, and in some places it may be a pre-Islamic tradition now "justified" by Islam.

I have a *chad'ri* myself, light blue, from my first trip to Mazar. I would probably not have bought it on my own, but another American had asked me to pick one up for his wife. The strong hint of naughty games in his tone struck a chord, and so I went to the *chad'ri* area of the bazaar with my translator and bought one for myself, too. I was disappointed when I tried it on. The tiny eyehole didn't allow for peripheral vision, the fabric was cheap nylon, and the color, while lovely, had no erotic resonances for me. It was wholesome rather than seductive in the way of the filmy black veils I'd seen in the United Arab Emirates and Jordan. But tastes in these matters differ.

When Amir asks me to put the *chad'ri* on I imagine it will be excitingly perverse to be wearing it for my Afghan lover, but once I slip it on I only feel uncomfortable. I look at Amir looking at me and raise my brows. Amir seems relieved when I quickly take it off. Maybe he was trying on a Western idea of what would be sexy and it didn't fit him. For his family the *chad'ri* would have shielded women from shame. It was not repressive, but protective, no more perverse than an umbrella in America. And much as I hated the *chad'ri* in Afghanistan, I felt as though I were kicking someone who was already down by mocking it in America.

Clothes are only the most visible sign of the gap between Afghan and Western ways. And it's very easy for a Westerner in Afghanistan to become preoccupied with the clothes themselves, rather than what they represent. It's even easier to simply condemn what one doesn't understand.

When I stayed in Mazar in November and taught English at Balkh University, I wore American clothes that approximated the local dress—a long coat over an ankle-length skirt over trousers. The filmy white head scarf I bought in the bazaar was more annoying. It always seemed in the way, and because the city was so dusty, I had to wash it nearly every day to maintain its pristine color. I could have worn a black scarf, but that is perceived as religiously conservative. Progressive women in the government and professions favor white or light-colored head scarves, so I did, too.

I tried hard to respect local values, although I would have felt better about wearing the head scarf had it been completely my choice. In some other Islamic countries I'd visited, I wore a scarf when there was no compulsion to do so and when some foreign women didn't. But here I had the feeling that I couldn't go out without the scarf, and I didn't like that. After all, I wasn't a Muslim, and the Quran does not say that non-believing women must cover their hair. It isn't even clear that it says that believing women must. But the covering of women has become absolutely central to Afghan life.

Trying to get a classroom conversation going one day among the overly quiet and respectful Balkh students, I ask what they'd buy their mothers if someone gave them twenty dollars to spend on a gift. I had learned to ask very open-ended questions—otherwise I would get canned answers like *I want to help rebuild my country* or *I want to become a doctor to help people.* They may, in fact, believe these things. However, as Dr. Sherif Fayez, the minister of higher education in Kabul, pointed out to me, there are seven doctors for every nurse in Afghanistan, because everyone wants to help in the most prestigious way possible. To know for sure how sincere the kids are, I would have to stay much longer, and I am only teaching English here for ten days, from noon to three every afternoon.

After I ask the question, my eyes go first to the girls, a cluster of gray and black on one side of the room, against the pale green walls.

Almost all of the young women answer, "a *chad'ri.*" It's a luxury item at ten dollars or so, and the thin nylon probably doesn't last long in this dusty, rough city. When I ask another group what improvements they would make here at the university, two of the four girls mention a changing room where they could put on their *chad'ri*s for the trip home.

It's a shock to me that these girls wear the *chad'ri;* I've never actually seen any of them take it off or put it on. But I've seen very, very few women in the street without them. The girls explained that it is too dangerous in a city fought over by warring factions in a simmering conflict that erupts into gun battles every few weeks. Any local thug calling himself a commander might take a fancy to an unveiled girl and demand her from her family. The family would be powerless to refuse unless they were highly connected. The only women you see without the *chad'ri* are the daughters of the powerful. Even Banu and Payman wear *chad'ri*s when they leave the house.

It's a big deal that the girls are here at all, in a classroom with young men, rather than already married and mothers, as most village girls of eighteen are. The resolutely progressive university administration is proud that nearly half the Balkh students are women. This is Dostum's influence; he started Balkh University and finances it. Still, these girls dress so that they barely register as physical presences. Their clothes are nunlike: black or gray tunics over long skirts of cheap synthetic fabrics and chadors; the more conservative ones' scarves are so tight and voluminous that they conceal every wisp of hair.

I know not to ask why they can't use the bathrooms to change.

There's running water only a few hours a day, and the three or four women's washrooms used by a thousand girls must be unbelievably dirty by the afternoon. But why don't they ask for more and better washrooms, or a better water supply, or more cleaners? The halls and classrooms are covered with dirt—not dust but dirt. It takes all my patience to refrain from saying, "Why don't you throw the *chad'ri*s out instead?"

A couple of weeks later, I am glad that I held my tongue. At the end of my trip, in Kabul, then–deputy women's minister Tajwar Kakar complains to me that the only topic female journalists from the West want to discuss is the veil. Kakar has returned from years of exile in Australia to take this job, but she wears traditional dress, including a head scarf. What she wants to talk about is job training and the encouragement of traditional cottage industries as a way of providing income for village women, but the women reporters aren't interested. "We are Muslim women and we are not going to dress like Europeans," she explains, and she wonders why foreigners can't get beyond this.

I know from the reading I've done about Afghanistan that Kakar is on to something. You would think from the reporting about Afghan women that the major problem they face is not poverty, or malnutrition, or lack of jobs or education, but whether or not to wear the *chad'ri*. Interest in other countries' customs is understandable, but this has the feel of an obsession.

It isn't till I read Germaine Tillion six months later that I'm able to put it in context. Although she discusses the veil and Islam, Tillion makes it clear that the related cultural phenom-

ena she is explaining—endogamy, particularly cousin marriage, and the seclusion of women—were as much a part of the
Christian southern Mediterranean as of the Arab lands across
the sea.

The purpose of veiling and the seclusion of women is to "keep
the girls in the family for the boys in the family" and thus
transmit property within the patriarchal clan. It has nothing
to do with Islam in Tillion's persuasive argument. Mohammed
was a social reformer in the context of seventh-century Arabia, and in contradiction to tribal Arabian practice, the Quran
insists that women inherit (at half of their brothers' portions,
because they are expected to be supported by their husbands).
This is why, Tillion noted in her research, endogamy in the
form of cousin marriage is more prevalent in Muslim bedouin
tribes where women, in fact, inherit. An interesting Web site,
consang.net, shows a world map with incidences of marriage
between relatives (consanguineous marriages). And today, the
greatest concentration of cousin marriage is in the Muslim
heartland ringing the Gulf states, where veiling also flourishes.

If I were an Afghan woman, I suspect I'd be furious at the insistence on veiling, even head scarves. I don't like being told
what to do. But I wonder why Western women—myself included—are bothered by a practice most Afghan women
wouldn't dream of abandoning. Why do we care more about
whether an Afghan woman covers her head than, say, whether
an Indian woman wears a sari? We make more of a fuss about
the head scarf than our gloved and hatted ancestors made
about the bare breasts of the women of Tahiti or Africa. That
Victorian outrage was an attempt to import the proprieties of
one society to another. Today we say it is evidence of repression,

the effort to stamp out in others what we suppressed in ourselves. Might our own outrage at the opposite phenomenon
be similar? Can it be the reminder of our former modesty that
infuriates Westerners?

It was not so long ago that American and European women
covered their heads. My mother, like most middle-class urban
women, would not have gone out in public in New York City
in the 1950s without a hat. Older southern European women
wore black scarves even after the Second World War and covered their heads in church until much more recently. Ortho-
dox Jewish women still wear wigs in public and hats as well;
many Jewish women cover their heads in synagogue. And then
there are the gloves worn by Western women in public until
about thirty-five years ago. I wore white gloves for dress occasions myself, as a little girl in the sixties. It was explained to
me as "good manners," but what was the deeper meaning of
the taboo on women showing their bare hands on formal occasions? Today journalists believe that women wearing gloves
in the Muslim world are practicing extreme *hijab,* and both
Shia Muslims and devout Sunni in many countries agree that
women's hands can be safely bared.

As for the seclusion of women, as recently as 1989 I found myself the only unaccompanied woman on the street in the *cen-
tro storico* of Palermo. It was still light, just before dinnertime.
There were hardly any couples, even in the good restaurants,
and no women in groups—not to mention alone. In France
you must go back another two generations, but apparently
the same was true in the southern areas; the great American
food writer M. F. K. Fisher wrote in the 1950s how she broke

the taboo on unaccompanied women dining out. Until the thirties in the United States, well-bred girls did not dine in public without a male family member or fiancé; even today a thirty-five-year-old Russian-born woman friend tells me that she will not go out to dinner with another woman unless they have a male escort.

Some of the Western fascination with and repulsion by the veil reflects our conflicted feelings about sexuality in general. One day toward the end of my stay in her house, Nabila asked me through Humayon about a bazaar rumor: Some foreigner had ordered sixty *chad'ri*s. "If they are so bad, why are the foreigners buying them?" I thought about how to respond. Nabila wore the *chad'ri* only in her immediate neighborhood, where the other women had not taken theirs off yet; in Mazar center she was comfortable in a head scarf. And she was proud of the photos of herself wearing a miniskirt as a young girl in Maimana in the seventies. So I explained that Westerners found *chad'ri*s very unusual and thought that they might become valuable years from now, when women in Afghanistan stopped wearing them. It might have even been the truth; the fellow who'd ordered them might be hoping to sell them in ten years for a hundred dollars each.

I was ashamed to give what I thought was likely the correct answer. I suspected that the foreigner buying *chad'ri*s in bulk was trading on the perverse implications of the garment for Westerners, who now find the restriction of women erotic precisely because our cultural rules tell us it's reprehensible. What other than this eros of restraint accounts for the mainstreaming of S & M that has placed handcuffs on the sales racks of

Sam Goody and black leather in malls? Now that there is general agreement that the control and restraining of women is a bad thing, we can mime it, and that's probably healthy.

Curled up in bed with Amir, I'm too happy to take the issues of dress very seriously. And when we finally leave my bedroom, I put on the green knickers, amused that they please him. After we finish eating the eggs we've cooked and Amir signals that we should go back to my bedroom, he reaches up to run his hands over the knickers' flowing drapery as I walk in front of him up the stairs. I can't imagine a better time than this.

And then he says, Have to practice getting used to these.

I bite my lip. I was starting to think of the knickers, like the food we cook, as one of the manifestations of the place we are creating together here, a blend of America and Afghanistan. But from time to time another reality intrudes into the night we have turned into day and the day we've turned into night. I'm afraid that Amir has a different picture of this blend, and I'm not in it, as he reminds me every so often—just when I feel closest to him and perhaps just when he feels closest to me.

13 | *foreign hands, part one*

On another cold February morning after a sleepless night of making love, Amir pulls on his jeans and T-shirt and says he should call his aunt in Texas. His cell phone shows a message from her in the middle of the night. Sometimes I think of breaking off relations with her, he says. She calls me too often.

This is the paternal aunt he said was like a second mother to him when he was a teenage refugee, the aunt who gave him one of the recipes we used at dinner the night before. Amir is close to some of his cousins, but a week after we first made love, some intuition made me ask how often he saw his parents. Once in the last fourteen years, he answered. This was shocking, but then his parents lived in Germany. He continued, I've told you about my immigrations issues. It's not so easy for me to leave the country. We talk on the phone, though.

I didn't want to hear what I suspected would be the answer, but I asked how often: Sometimes every couple of weeks, sometimes every few months.

I didn't say anything, but I must have looked disapproving. I know his culture; I know how close Afghan families are. The paternal aunt is a special figure. When a man marries, his wife usually moves in with his family, and their children grow up with his sisters as surrogate mothers. I saw it in the way that Banu and Seema and Payman took care of Loulou and Siddiq. I try to picture Siddiq thirty years from now, complaining that Banu calls him too often. Was Amir a monster? Or was I a prig to gasp when he told me a truth he could easily have concealed, making the effort to show me his real self? Who was I to judge? Until my mother became frail in her seventy-sixth year, I saw her no more than once or twice a month, and she lived only an hour's drive away. I haven't seen my three aunts in decades, ever since my mother feuded with them, and aside from Thanksgiving and Passover dinners, I don't see my mother's cousins regularly. If I were honest with myself, I'd admit I admired Amir's society for a closeness I have turned away from in my own culture.

When Amir spoke of breaking off with his aunt, I remembered something Shirin had told me, which Amir had repeated when we talked about marrying relatives. Amir didn't talk to one of his three brothers in Germany because he'd married an Iranian. Yet he spoke tenderly of *the little brother I helped to raise. I carried him around on my shoulders.* I picture Siddiq and Loulou. What was the problem, I asked; his brother's wife was a Muslim, after all, and Amir admitted she was from a good family. It's tradition, he said. She's not an Afghan.

I've never been very close to my own and only brother, and we've had terrible arguments, but the idea of never talking with him again frightens me to death. The idea of never talking again with anyone I've loved frightens me to death. Amir doesn't even know if he has little nieces and nephews: My parents know not to mention my brother to me, he says. What is my claim on Amir compared to his brother's or his aunt's? I could easily be next. And so I say nothing when he speaks of breaking off with his aunt. I am like Sheherezad in reverse. As long as I am silent I have a chance of keeping things going.

I hear Amir mumbling on the phone in Pashtu. When he comes back his face is grave. His cousin had a heart attack and is in intensive care. He lights a cigarette and says, I'm glad I called. It's so sad—he's only thirty; he was married just a year ago. I mean, I'm single. If something happens to me . . . so what? Amir shrugs, sits down on the couch, motions to me to join him.

Does he mean that his life is worthless until he is married? Is Amir speaking from self-pity, hoping I'll protest that if something happened to him I'd be heartbroken? This is true, and I want to tell him I adore him, but I stop myself. If he can talk of breaking off with his aunt because she wants to be close to him, he can just as easily jettison me for the same reason. Before I can think about it more, he's pulling me to him and peeling off the T-shirt and drawstring pants I just put on.

In the afternoon, I try to interest Amir in watching *Blade Runner,* the first DVD I bought for my first-ever TV and DVD player. It's the director's cut, I say. It's a little different from the original version.

What's *Blade Runner*?

When *Blade Runner* came out in 1982, I was working on Wall Street, and Amir was a fourteen-year-old living outside Herat, dreaming of touching a pair of polyester knickers.

It's a very famous American movie. It's about a love affair between a kind of android passing as human, what they call a replicant, and the man who is supposed to hunt her down and kill her. And there's a question about whether he might be a replicant himself.

Oh, it's science fiction? I don't like science fiction.

Well, it's based on a Philip K. Dick novella. He's terrific; he's not just a science fiction writer.

I'd written an *Artforum* essay years before in which I argued that *Blade Runner* was an allegory of race relations in the United States, that the issue of "passing" and the question of what it is to be considered fully human were questions that absorbed Dick in common with many people in sixties America. And I was coming to think that Amir felt about Afghans very much as Deckard and the other blade runners felt about humans, and that he saw Americans as the blade runners saw replicants. Then again, some Americans saw him as an alien, which legally he was. I couldn't tell if the prodigies he performed in bed were despite or because I was in some ways alien to him. *He doesn't really trust Americans,* Shirin had commented, and I thought of how my great-uncles had told me I could never trust a non-Jew.

Amir lets me begin the movie, but he's restive, maybe intentionally so. After fifteen minutes or so, the phone rings, and I pause the film to answer the call. When I rejoin him on the couch we start making love again and the movie is forgotten.

Then Amir gives me a short Dari lesson, and at the end, I playfully ask him, Write me some dirty words. I want to know the words for pussy, ass, fuck me. He hesitates, and when he begins to write *kouss, koon, man rah begou* in Arabic script, he's red with embarrassment.

Amir, I say softly, I can't believe you're blushing.

I think I've never written those words before. You must know, one is a different person in different languages . . .

I remember our first Dari lesson, when he asked me, *Voulez-vous coucher avec moi ce soir?* I understand now why he spoke in French. Amir was less ashamed to talk of sex in that language. Even English was too close to home for him.

This has something to do with his native language, too. In Farsi, I'm learning, there's a huge gap between the spoken, or colloquial, and the written, or formal, language—narrowed only by some innovative novelists. Generally you don't write the same verb forms you say. In Iran, TV newscasters use formal rather than colloquial Farsi, and so do politicians. In a culture with this gap, writing the words for the most private of acts is momentous. The same is true for Arabic; some Western commentators think this is part and parcel of the estrangement of ordinary Arabs from their mainly corrupt and unjust governments, whose official communications are lies.

I don't share Amir's feeling about being a different person

when speaking different languages. I feel a little stagy in my scanty but decent-sounding Italian and a little crude in my strong but badly accented French, but my feelings about sex or politics or family don't change from language to language. I was interviewed in French about my first book a few months earlier, and the conversation felt relatively transparent from my end (what the interviewer felt about my accent might have been another matter). But I don't know French as well as Amir knows English or Farsi or Pashtu; I'm not anywhere close to bilingual. The only time I feel like another person in another language is when I write Farsi or Arabic—when I take pen in hand.

When I first began studying Farsi with Shirin—by coincidence, two nights after I met Amir, in June 2002—I told her I wanted not only to speak the language but to learn to read and write it. She was delighted to hear that I was interested in the riches of Persian literature and spoke eagerly of a future in which we read the great Persian poets Rumi and Hafez together.

Shirin was not the kind of teacher I had in mind when I advertised at NYU for an Afghan Dari teacher. Just back from my first trip to Afghanistan, I envisioned a serious, somewhat elderly intellectual refugee, perhaps a woman who'd taught college. It hadn't occurred to me that in a country with 90 percent female illiteracy, such a woman had probably been asked to be a minister in Karzai's government. At any rate, no Afghans applied, just Shirin.

Shirin looks a bit like Farah Diba and a bit like the young Jackie Kennedy. Short and energetic, she's a painter of great ambition but playful and charming enough not to be overbearing. She fled Iran with her aristocratic family after elementary school, so her book learning in Farsi is limited but more than adequate for teaching a beginner. She has a musician's ear and voice and an artist's hand at calligraphy. As soon as we advanced beyond the point of letter recognition, Shirin surprised me with a gift: a tiny bottle of black ink, a large drawing pad, and a bamboo pen she carved for me herself. "Now you're going to learn to write beautiful Persian," she said.

I stared at Shirin. I was so surprised that I forgot that this was impossible, that my handwriting had always been terrible, even in English. Because my family moved around a lot when I was in the first few years of elementary school, I never learned to write cursive well; I still print today. My bad penmanship was a source of mild shame in school. I maintained to my teachers that it was the content, not the appearance, of my writing that was important, and my grades were good enough to get away with it most of the time. But I was embarrassed about the way my handwriting looked, and as personal computers became widespread, I happily reduced writing in longhand to the bare minimum of birthday cards and thank-you notes.

Today I am so unaccustomed to writing by hand that my fingers ache after half an hour of taking notes. Until now it had never occurred to me to improve the appearance of my handwriting. Even when I spent much of my time in college studying ancient Greek, I'd never cared about how my handwriting looked. How ironic that the one language I might someday have good handwriting in could be Persian, my eighth foreign language.

I have a long history with other scripts—Biblical Hebrew when I was a child and ancient Greek in college—but until fall 2001, I never saw a reason to learn Farsi. It didn't look too likely that I'd be traveling to Iran or Afghanistan any time soon. And while I always knew that Farsi had a great poetic tradition, the only Persian poets I'd sampled, the eleventh-century Omar Khayyám and the thirteenth-century Sufi Rumi, didn't appeal to me in the flowery English translations I'd seen. It was only after 9/11 and our defeat of the Taliban that going to Afghanistan looked like a possibility. And only after I'd read a lot of sloppy American news coverage of the war did it occur to me that relying on translators meant missing a lot. As I got more interested in Middle Eastern politics, I thought about learning Farsi and, if that took, Arabic.

Even for someone who loves learning new languages, this was not enough in the way of motivation. The emotional impetus had to do with the script. For as long as I could recall, I'd thought the Arabic script in which Persian is written the loveliest I'd ever seen. Persian is an Indo-European language, while Arabic is Semitic, but the Arabs who conquered Persia in the seventh and eighth centuries brought their writing to the Persians. I admired it in Persian miniatures, on tenth-century Iraqi pottery, in old Qurans. While traveling in Java at twenty-six, I bought a huge old blue and white Sumatran batik full of squiggles and swirls that my brother, who did a year of college Arabic, said were the first verses of the Quran. I hung it in my dining room. I loved its flourishes and vaguely mused about someday learning to read them.

Learning to write even halfway decent Persian proved much harder than learning to speak the language. I paid attention to the minute details of letter forming for the first time since I learned to write English. I was learning calligraphy, and there were many styles to choose from. It took me time to figure out the aesthetics and to decipher words and phrases I already knew. Then there were purely mechanical problems: I wrote inconsistently, I couldn't make the same letter the same way every time, I had scale problems relating letters to one another. These defects make a nonnative English speaker's handwriting stand out immediately. But until I tackled Farsi calligraphy, it never occurred to me how hard it was to get it right. Sometimes it wasn't a matter of an error: Shirin just told me what I'd written was ugly.

I didn't react impatiently, as I did when I was a child learning English penmanship. I was willing to submit to this discipline, though I couldn't expect to be accomplished at it for many years, if ever. Persian culture took handwriting as an indicator of cultural level. To have beautiful handwriting meant that one was a cultivated person, and I accepted that as the price of admission to a new world.

Another cold winter morning Amir comes back from a dawn cigarette run smiling shyly, and hands me a solitary red rose, saying in a low voice, I did the Jewish thing and only got you one.

I reach up, mime a slap, kiss him instead. The bedraggled Korean deli rose in its stiff plastic casing looks as if it will die in the next few minutes if it isn't put in water—or maybe anyway.

I never would have bought it. Amir doesn't know this, but I sometimes joke to friends that I'm too Jewish to buy cut flowers, since they last for so short a time. So his Jewish slur hurts a little, but it amuses me, too. And Amir did tell me early on, *I majored in Jewish girls in college. I'm not sure why—maybe being outsiders, we had something in common.*

The last man to give me a deli rose had been Dave, a boyfriend briefly and then a friend for years. In some ways Amir reminded me of him: charming, shy, but the life of the party

when he was a little drunk; said to be fiercely intelligent by his
friends, a claim substantiated by his sparkling eyes but not by
much of our time together. Dave told me that he loved me
when it was too late, and too late for me to answer in kind, as
I'd wanted to. The deli rose had come much earlier, in the few
months when we still desired each other.

The Victorians had a language of flowers of which but one law
remains: a man only gives a red rose to a woman he desires.
The red is not only for the heart and for passion but for blood
and death. Flowers accompany romance not just for their
beauty and scent but for their transcience. Cut roses die fast,
cheap ones faster, and these deli roses arrive nearly finished.
But that is part of their appeal, at least to the men who buy
them, half ironically, for me. Another aspect is their studied
casualness, the "I just happened to pick this up" impression,
so far from the solemn duty of buying a girlfriend flowers.
Amir added the tiny barb about Jewish thrift to make sure I
wouldn't think he was sappy, and he had reason to be cautious. I'd crisply told him his preference for the Beatles over
the Stones showed sentimentality, and I'd looked at him
askance when he asked me if I had bubble bath. But secretly I
adored the corniness that escaped his censorship.

My friend Jason—the one who said Amir was a savage even if
he had gone to Princeton—also said, "Cruel cultures are sentimental." There was truth in this. Just as in Samuel's declara-
tion that people are nicer in the Third World because they
have to be: Without the rule of law, without decent governments, there are only the bonds of family and kindness to ce-
ment society. That might be why so many of my friends are
from the Third World—they are nice. But it also makes sense

the other way around. Sentimental cultures are also cruel, as a matter of self-protection. The guilelessness and depth of feeling that melted my heart in Afghanistan require a shield; such sentiment only flourishes, it might be, because it is defended by rigid rules, arranged marriages, and an inexorable honor code.

Sentimental cultures are also cultures where men are still sure of their authority. Amir could express a liking for Barry White that would have raised eyebrows among his WASP eating-club friends because he had fought in a war while they were sailing and playing tennis. Amir's unreconstructed masculinity allowed him to be more tender and expressive than the men I was used to; it allowed him to let me see him cry. He was certain that being a man was worth something, and American men have lost that assurance.

Not that Afghan society is a simple patriarchy. Once Amir told me that when he got married, he intended to be the head of the household, unlike his older brothers, whom he thought were dominated by their cousin-wives. I refrained from telling him that many anthropologists have concluded that Afghan society is as matriarchal within the house as it is patriarchal outside. As a twentysomething Afghan intellectual told me in Kabul, "I am afraid of displeasing my father. But I am terrified of displeasing my mother. For an Afghan, the worst thing is the anger of your mother."

I took pleasure in deferring to Amir as a man and humoring his enactment of Afghan men's and women's roles—he bought the groceries, I cleaned up—which felt harmless and fun. When he suggested that I read the fourth sura of the Quran to understand how wonderful Islam really is about women, I didn't tell him that I found it as banal as similar sections of the Torah. It helped that there were contradictions in his attitude, that he loved to cook, and I saw him cry before I let him see my tears. It was he who raised the issue of these roles, asking as I cleaned up after dinner one night, Should I pretend to be a sensitive man and ask if you need help? At twenty-four I would have been outraged if Scott hadn't helped as a matter of course. But the intervening twenty years had taught me something, and I meant it when I smiled and told Amir, Of course not, you are my guest.

Even before Amir entered my life, I'd started to believe that much of what modern American women feel is missing in their men—tender courtship behavior, gallantry, and emotional bravery—flourishes when men are sure of their authority and not when they are on the defensive. Anglo-American courtship in the eighteenth and nineteenth centuries was a role reversal, a saturnalia in which men were able to play at being submissive and humble before women because everyone knew quite well that the truth was the reverse. Yet women today both expect formal equality and the gestures that flourish only in its absence.

Equality is a noble political principle, but it works far better within groups than between two people. Within large groups the principle of equality seems to promote stability, because no one scrutinizes power dynamics so closely as to become concerned with minor differences. One-on-one, where such comparisions are unavoidable, tiny differences assume outsize importance. No one is pleased.

When you've been with a lover for a few years or more, you see the pitfalls of looking too hard at equality. One person becomes fixated on the perception that the couple spends more time with the other person's friends or family, or gives more value to the other's tastes or preferences. Before you know it, having potatoes rather than rice with dinner becomes an example of selfishness or coercion. The more you believe in equality as an ideology, the more dissatisfied you become with the unavoidable, if small, unfairnesses in everyday life.

Resentment at these small differences leads to hypersensitivity to slights to the ego. We're quick to retaliate in order to preserve the all-important concept of a level playing field. A woman cancels a date at the last minute because she has to work late—well, to show that he is no less important, the man in question takes his time in returning her call. A husband won't attend his wife's college reunion—so she won't accompany him to the important client dinner. A man e-mails a woman that he's too busy to see her for a week or so—and she has to do something similar to keep the balance of power. Young women keep track of how many times the men they live with put the dishes in the dishwasher, and young husbands wait to see how long it takes their wives to ask how the meeting went.

I've been guilty of every error I mention. If I can be more re-laxed and kinder now, some of the reason is a self-assurance I didn't have in my twenties. When Victorian men's authority allowed them to be tender, women's corresponding confi-dence in their own worth—derived from their socially recog-nized and valued role as wives and mothers—allowed them to be graciously deferential.

This is not to subscribe to the popular cliché that men can't stand smart, powerful women. To the contrary, mating in the United States and similar countries is what economists call highly assortive—like with like, well-educated, high-earning men with their female counterparts. The reason some men seek women who are much less powerful than they are is that with them they feel enough authority to be tender. They aren't looking for weak women—just for women next to whom they feel strong. Rather than complaining about this, we could try understanding it. Maybe this trait serves a purpose. The dignity it bestows on men can make them behave more lovingly to their wives and children. Their tenderness is greatest where their confidence in their own authority is also greatest.

Part of the problem is that the entire area of love and marriage and family life has been devalued in our culture. Nineteenth-century American men valued marriage. They would press their fiancées for shorter engagement periods and quicker marriages, while women (afraid of childbirth and household drudgery) preferred to draw out the time before marriage. In fact, until the late nineteenth or early twentieth century, a successful marriage and family life was considered the pinnacle of male as well as female aspirations in the West, as it still is in Afghanistan. A man's career did not exist in a vacuum; the point of earning money was to provide a home for his family, and this family became the center of his emotional life, as it was of his wife's. Having a stable, well-run, happy home increased a man's prestige, just as having a thriving, well-run business did. Men found in the respect of their wives, children, and household servants the support and also the ego boost that they now look for at the office. And they gave back to them the protective tenderness, practical concern, and emotional involvement we're now told men are "naturally" not set up to manage.

It's become fashionable lately to argue that men aren't wired for marriage or even for intimacy. According to this view, biological differences are to blame:

> Because the male brain is devoting more cortical areas to spatials, it tends to devote less cortical areas to word use and word production than the female. This is why a man will tend to spend his free time tossing a football or playing a video game, whereas a woman might chat on the phone or curl up with a book . . . Men have a more difficult time making language out of experience than women do. In fact, they use, on average, about half the amount of words that women do. (Michael Gurian, *What Could He Be Thinking?* 2003)

Some of my women friends eat this sort of thing up, and I haven't always been immune to its seductions, but more and more it gives me pause. I've never read about eighteenth-century European men spending any time at all tossing a football or playing video games. Novels of the period suggest that well-off men spent a lot of leisure time in drawing rooms talking or alone in their studies reading or writing letters to friends, family, and lovers. In Afghanistan adult men do not seem to play sports at all, except for the rare burly fellow who plays *buzkashi*, Afghan polo; video games are unknown. And if men use half the words women do, isn't it peculiar that up until the late eighteenth century, nearly all great works of literature sprang from the pens of this handicapped sex?

My skepticism about the biological basis of intimacy became

disdain when I read some recent scholarship on Victorian American courtship. Love letters are one of the main historical sources for ordinary people's feelings because they tend to be preserved and passed down, and I found excerpts from hundreds of Victorian love letters in books by Karen Lystra and Claudia Rothman. As I read, I had trouble believing that the tender and unabashedly devoted letters were by the same men Gurian described:

> O happy hours when I may once more encircle within these arms the dearest object of my love . . . when I may again press to my heart which palpitates with the purest affection the loved one who has so long shared its undivided devotion. (1842)

> How intensely do I long to see you—to *feel* you—to put these hands that hold this pen upon you. Yes in your bosom—that soft delicious bosom. I shall tear you to pieces. (1834)

And, written by a husband to his wife of fifteen years:

> I think of you every day, and every hour of the day, and almost every minute of the hours. (1852)

The idea that men are emotionally disabled compared with women doesn't agree with this kind of historical evidence. Nor does the effort to find a biological basis for their alleged shortcomings. Surely male brain chemistry hasn't changed in 150 years. The denigration of male emotion is popular because it helps explain the more general failure of many Americans to feel, as well as the tendency of both men and women to intellectualize their emotions and valorize managing relationships rather than falling in love.

Rather than admit to a terrible problem in the culture at large, it's easier to point the finger at one sex. Now it's fashionable to condemn men; at other times women were considered deficient in some key regard. So we look for scientific grounds to pronounce men less emotional, less expressive, less human— and ignore several thousand years of cultural history that argues otherwise. Those who are eager to point to brain differences fail to notice basic structural differences between our society and our ancestors'.

If men no longer view marriage as positively as their ancestors did, it's not just because they have an easier time getting premarital sex, as a certain crude level of thought would have it. (American statistics show that most Victorian men had premarital sex, just not with the women they eventually wed, while women who had premarital sex mainly had it with the men they later married.) It's because the institution provided emotional rewards it no longer does. Men haven't changed, women haven't changed, but the institution has.

Women are not to blame for being nostalgic for old-fashioned romance; the traditional forms were beautiful and satisfying. What woman today doesn't want a man to pursue her tenderly and persistently and imaginatively? But women can't have their cake and eat it, too. How many women would do what their great-grandmothers did to call forth this behavior? How many are capable of the deference, gratitude, and submission that their great-grandfathers took for granted in a wife? Outside this dynamic, it is infinitely harder for a man to put himself at the mercy of the woman he loves.

We've lost the structure that made Victorian courtship gracious and satisfying, and that helped Victorian marriages endure. What's left are the stray symbols, which loom larger now that the rest of the culture has dissolved: the red rose, Valentine's Day, the engagement ring, the white dress. And people with any kind of individual sensibility are embarrassed by them, even as they're secretly moved—because they evoke a world we miss, no matter how much we scorn it.

Nearly every Valentine's Day I've been with a boyfriend, I've had a fight. The stress of having appropriate emotions and buying appropriate gifts sinks any natural pleasure not already squeezed out of the holiday by its tacky commercialism. So I'm determined not to spend the evening with Amir. The problem is that Shirin is having an opening, and she wants both of us to come. Amir might feel the same way about the holiday as I do, because he e-mailed me that he might run into me at the opening. I don't know which is worse—his lack of an explicit invitation or the fact that I don't want to go anyway, yet feel I have to.

I decide to arrive late, hoping to miss Amir. Samuel has the flu, so I have the excuse of keeping Rebecca company. But when I arrive just before the closing, Amir is planted squarely by the entrance to the gallery, conveniently close to the bar. He offers me a glass of wine; he seems to have had quite a few already.

I want to be cool, but I find myself kissing him lustily on the lips, and the moment I do it I'm afraid he'll be annoyed at the public display of affection. But he seems very happy to see me.

What are you doing later? he mumbles.

Just here for a minute, I answer.

I have plans with Rebecca and Luisa and Jason, but I wanted to stop by and see Shirin's work. And I do force myself to leave fifteen minutes later. Since we started dating it's the only time I've seen Amir without making love with him.

On Sunday morning it's snowing heavily, and there is nothing I like so much as spending days like this in bed with a man. I leave a message for Amir. He doesn't call me back until the evening. I just got up, he tells me. I'm relieved; I'd thought he was trying my patience, or even, heartbreakingly, in bed with someone else.

He continues: I had a late night, I went to sleep at five, and I'm not feeling so good. I'm going to drink some green tea and see how that goes down. I'll come over later if I feel better.

I go to Rebecca and Samuel's house to hang out with Rebecca and don't get home till one in the morning. There's a forlorn-sounding message from Amir on my machine: *It's eleven now. I fell asleep again; I just got up. I could come over, but you're not home. I guess I'll go back to bed.*

When we speak the next day, Washington's Birthday, at noon, Amir tells me he slept for twenty-seven hours, with a few hours of wakefulness here and there: I took an Ambien at eleven thirty when I realized you weren't home.

I tell him, You're living like there's no tomorrow.

He ignores my remark. Let's make *aash*. It's a good day for it.
I'll bring the special ingredients.

Aash is my favorite Afghan food, a thick Uzbek soup that was
served often at Nabila's house and at Amir's childhood home
by their Uzbek cook.

Amir invites me to have brunch with some of his friends first,
but I say I have work to do. The truth is, I'm still wary of seeing him with other people around.

Then he adds, And if I remember, I'll bring you some of my
books. Maybe something about Afghanistan. Or Clausewitz's
On War—have you read that?

No. I'd like to though. Clausewitz has been in the air this
spring, as the U.S. invasion of Iraq draws closer to reality.

Amir calls twice from the restaurant to find out what spices I
have. He sounds cranky when he insists, I won't make it if
I can't find dried mint. And when he tells me he's had a couple
of margaritas, I decide I was right not to meet him at the
restaurant.

Instead, I shovel a foot and a half of snow from the sidewalk
outside my house, which as a property owner I'm legally responsible for clearing. The exercise helps dissolve the tension that's
been growing as I wonder what kind of mood Amir will be in.

But when Amir walks down the path I've just shoveled carrying the groceries, he is happy and relaxed. His skin glows and his eyes sparkle, and his luxuriant hair, a little shorter now, falls just right on his forehead. His freshness reminds me of our age difference.

You got a good haircut.

Yeah, I paid double what I normally pay. It cost me twelve dollars. I felt like a woman! And he looks coyly at me, as he always does when he makes a remark he knows many American women would bristle at. But I find his efforts at provocation so charming, I always laugh.

We have to take pictures of each other in the snow before we start cooking. You don't realize, I explain, it only snows like this once every ten years.

Since the camera is digital I can see them immediately: Amir wildly happy, grinning in the middle of the street opposite my house; me tired and worried, standing with a snow shovel in front of my door.

I was anxious not just because I couldn't predict Amir's mood but because I didn't want him to ruin a perfect day. I love it when the snow lies in drifts like this, as deep as I can remember it in New York. It reminds me of my early childhood, of the happier days in Pennsylvania before my father was diagnosed with Parkinson's disease. Then my father was a dependable protector, not an invalid I had to tiptoe around. He used to make soup sometimes on winter days. Unlike my mother, he enjoyed cooking, and as the breadwinner he had the luxury of doing it only when he wanted to. I can just dimly picture him in a rough wool Pendleton shirt, gray wool pants, and incongruous black dress socks, working in the kitchen. When I was six he would have been thirty-eight—what I would now think of as a youngish man, just a little older than Amir is now. I can't remember those afternoons, really, but I remember the taste of the soup vividly. It was called Daddy soup, not *aash*, but many of the ingredients were the same.

As Amir sets to work, I see that my fears are groundless. Amir is relaxed and happy. He tells me to brown some onions in peanut oil while he washes the carrots and potatoes, then explains that we should chop them into large, crude pieces. We don't use cutting boards in Afghanistan—did you notice that when you were there? We cut in our hands. But I don't do that. I decided to introduce an innovation, he adds, producing a lone turnip. And we're going to use canned chickpeas. I'm sure they didn't do that when you were there. And we shouldn't put in too many tomatoes, just a few. What's that ground meat for? I don't remember that.

Tiny lamb meatballs, they're the best. That's what my family used. I mean the family I stayed with, I correct, hoping he won't comment on the slip. Amir doesn't remember meat in the soup, but I've had it a lot more recently than he has, and I get my way.

By chance I have just the right spoons, Russian papier-mâché, which Nabila also used. Amir says they are a local status symbol. Did you know that in the villages, they don't even have those? They use very primitive carved wooden spoons.

The soup is finished quickly and we eat just after dark. Then we spend the rest of the afternoon and evening making love on my couch in the living room, the windows to the street shrouded with thick scarves, the usual traffic noise silenced by the snowfall.

At midnight, Amir puts on his clothes to leave. He has to be at work at eight, and after one night of insomnia, he's abandoned the attempt to spend the night at my house on work nights. This makes me sad, but it pales next to the thought that he's leaving for Afghanistan. That talk of bringing over his books makes me think it's happening soon, though he's never specific.

As Amir gets his coat on, my cats make a tentative reappearance. Amir is allergic, and though this usually makes the cats crowd perversely round a visitor, they sense something different about him. They disappear when he's in the house. They don't even nest in his thick wool coat, usually just the sort of fabric they delight in covering with hairs.

You treat my cats like furniture, I say, and Amir smiles: But I don't step on them, do I? Then he brags to me that he enjoyed dog and camel fights when he was a small boy. When I ask if he likes animals at all, Amir says he loves dogs.

It's the last thing I expect, for dogs are *haram*, prohibited, and in traditional Muslim cultures they aren't allowed in the house. I've seen that in the Middle East, not only dogs but even cats are considered unclean. A Turkish friend of mine, thoroughly cosmopolitan, was horrified at the thought of a kitten in her apartment. Judaism doesn't go so far as to declare dogs unclean, as Islam does, but I remember my father joking, "the less Jewish the household, the more dogs." I was never allowed a pet growing up because my mother thought animals were dirty. Her aversion, I decided after travel in the Middle East, was probably cultural as much as personal. It surprised me many years later when she grew to love my cats.

I adopted Kimba one warm June day in 1990 when he rubbed against my bare foot in the garden of my East Village apartment—a tiny black kitten I at first feared was a rat. Soon he was joined by Dink, a painfully thin tortoiseshell stray who put on so much weight as to make a joke of her name. My mother was right. They did make a mess. Cat hair became a permanent fixture on my clothing and on the upholstered furniture. Finding someone to take care of Kimba and Dink when I traveled was a constant problem. And I had a surprising ability to find friends and lovers who were allergic to cats.

But even after Kimba had grown out of his cute kitten tricks, I couldn't imagine life without animals in the house. It was hard to put a finger on why I enjoyed their presence, but other people liked Kimba and Dink, too. Friends who'd house-sat asked after the cats years later. And even my mother petted them lovingly when she visited and often asked how they were.

One day I told her that I'd never have guessed she'd take to them. She answered, "Oh, they're very cute. As long as I don't have to take care of them, I like seeing them from time to time. And they've been good for you." I asked what she meant by that. "Well, it's nice to see your tenderness to animals. I think that's the first time you've been able to relate to beings that aren't intelligent."

This brought me up short. She was right. Intellectual admiration is an unspoken requirement for my friendship, my love, and even for desire that burns beyond a few nights. Most of all, it has been a feature of my family life. Our family is small and, luckily for my prejudices, smart; I name my brother and mother among the brightest people I know. And our way of relating to one another has always been verbal and explicit. We don't make small talk; we don't hug and kiss much; we don't sit around in silence just enjoying one another's company, as—to my surprise—I hear that some families do.

Around the time of this conversation with my mother, I was starting to worry about my romantic—as opposed to my sexual—life. It hardly existed. There were men I enjoyed going to bed with, some of whom I found intellectually engaging, too, but there wasn't much of an emotional connection. If I were honest with myself, I rarely felt anything besides a bruised ego when these affairs were over. I doubt the men felt more. It was very rare for me to feel an emotional bond with a man before I went to bed with him. Besides Scott, I could only think of a handful of examples.

It was hard for me to think of any living being that I related to mainly on an emotional level, for whom my tenderness wasn't based on admiration and a conversational connection. I assumed that if I'd had children, this would have been different; I would have had an emotional bond with them long before they could talk. But the first children I found captivating were Loulou and Siddiq, and I was already forty-four when I met them.

When I daydreamed that winter about a future with Amir, our difference in age loomed far more ominously for me than our difference in background. It wasn't just the fact that I had to have a child soon or not at all, while in my view, Amir wasn't close to being ready for fatherhood. It was in a lot of little things, like the way he was still surrounded by his Princeton crowd, the way he spoke about the joys of "partying," the many experiences he hadn't had that were already old for me. But at the same time, our ten-year gap in age went some way toward making our romance possible.

It was a tremendous thrill knowing that Amir, at thirty-four, was as crazy about me physically as I was about him. At forty-four I could see signs of decay in my body even if he could not, even if those who saw us together could not. But most of what I have enjoyed about being with younger men, including him, hasn't been reassurance about my looks. The real joy is in being able to be more emotionally generous. Because it isn't so deadly serious, because I don't think in terms of marrying

these men, because I'm not trying so hard, I can be the flex-
ible, reasonable, and solicitious woman that I wish I were all
the time.

When I was in my twenties I mainly dated older men, men in
their thirties or early forties; I say "older" though I don't think
anyone was as old as I am now. Sometime in my early thirties I
crossed over to dating younger men. The first was Dave, who
had given me my first deli rose. He was eight years my junior.
And as I reached my forties, I realized that I'd been dating
younger men for almost a decade.

Romances across the years were an ongoing topic for banter,
not only with many of my male friends but with my women
friends, too. And I'd come to see some commonalities among
us. Many of my friends who date much younger people have
never married, or have married very briefly, and have no children. It's obvious even to us that we have our issues, both with
our parents and with our own generation. We older partners
may be able to be kinder, wiser, or more seductive when it isn't
serious (or we think it isn't), as it allows us to relax long
enough to let the relationship happen. With younger partners,
we're more tolerant. It's easier to excuse someone who's nearly
young enough to be your child for behaving like a kid; it's easier not to take acting out personally when it's sketched in such
broad strokes. And we may be more willing to forgive as we realize how many of our trespasses were forgiven when we were
young.

To take off on the famous one-liner about Jews, love between
people far apart in years is just like other kinds of love, only
more so. It lends itself to dramatizing our confusions about

family, both the family in which we were raised and any family we might wish to create. There's an oedipal element in these affairs, as in all love. This displacement of family feelings may have something to do with the tendency of some older people to date younger partners they have to take care of emotionally or even financially and who cannot in return take care of them. But much of what we seek in them isn't that simple. In fact, they're more meaningful and more appealing as conventional family structure dissolves.

It used to be that affairs with partners much younger or older paid tribute to generally acknowledged notions of appropriate couplings by flouting them. Their frisson came from their forbidden quality and from the eroticism of differences. But now American and European families are slipping out of their patriarchal moorings. Gender roles and the meaning of adulthood are both blurring. Gay marriage is under debate; half of all marriages end in divorce; 34 percent of American children are born out of wedlock. In this new context, making love across the generations—are the parameters ten years, fifteen, twenty?—becomes a way of exploring what we want from family and community, rather than a way of defying them, a search for connection and meaning rather than a relief from them.

Some of what we're increasingly looking for in all of our romances, no matter the age of the partners, is the traditional, intact society the historian Peter Laslett poetically termed, "the world we have lost." I am not the only one to long for the tenderness and natural pleasure in domestic life that still echoes here and there in the stories told by our immigrant grandparents or great-grandparents. We miss the firm grounding in

our age group and the bond of tenderness across the generations that arises naturally in traditional societies, where marriage and child rearing are nearly universal, age and gender
roles are well defined, and children and parents of whatever
ages live together—often literally—in relative harmony. We
miss it as much as we dread it.

Affairs between people far apart in age are, among other
things, a way to recover this warmth and heal the wounds in-
flicted by our birth families. Most of the younger men I've
been with, and many of the younger women or men dating my
friends, have had difficult or unusual relationships with their
families. Many lost parents early in life, were raised by single
mothers, or left home in their midteens. Dave is at the other
extreme, still living with his parents in his late thirties, though
he can well afford not to. More are like Amir. They haven't
seen their parents in years, or they pay infrequent duty visits.
I can think offhand of a half dozen men who've dated older
women—my exes, friends' boyfriends—who only call their parents every few months and see them less frequently than that.

Mortality enters into every love, but it's sharper when there's
a big difference in age. Some of my tenderness for my older
lovers' bodies came from knowing their fragility. I knew it
more strongly when I was with an older man. I couldn't stop
thinking, *He'll die before me.* It seemed a steep price to pay for
the wisdom and sophistication and money and power he had
over me. I would pity him for his mortality if for nothing else,
pity him even if he had no pity for me.

It's a shock to realize that some of these men are in their sixties now. By chance I saw the picture of one of those old lovers

recently in a business publication; he looked like a grand-father—white beard and genial smile. Yet in my mind he's still thirty-seven to my twenty-two, and he's still telling me to read each day's *Wall Street Journal* and *New York Times* cover to cover, even if I have to save them till the weekend. How tall would the pile of those newspapers stand now, twenty-three years later?

Affairs between younger and older partners are innately risky, insisting on chemistry rather than logic, the moment rather than the long run, difference rather than similarity, the erotic rather than the practical. The attempt to reach across the most intractable of barriers—time—intensifies the emotional bond. These affairs can be what anthropologist Clifford Geertz called "deep play," theaters in which we act out the dramas most crucial for us. And the first and most emotional is that of family, with taking our place in the roster of generations.

Some of the emotional generosity I tried to give to Amir might have gone, if my life had taken different turns, to a son instead. And some of what he took from me, I'd grown to suspect, was what he felt was denied him by his parents and by the cruelties of politics and history. Love across the generations always carries a whiff of the unnatural, but it can also heal the injuries of time and restore to us the tenderness we believe is our due.

Shirin is standing outside the bar when I arrive, shivering against the early March wind in a too-thin vintage black leather coat. I thought she would be inside with Amir, but she explains that he's pretty messed up—being childish, ignoring her, flirting with the waitresses. "You might want to skip it, Ann. I don't know."

But I haven't seen Amir in two weeks, and he did e-mail me suggesting that we get together tonight. The original plan was for him to have a drink with Shirin and maybe bring her with him over to my house to say hello. This party was a later addition.

Shirin wanted to talk with Amir about an offer she's received from my friend Robert, a well-known journalist: if she helps Robert get a visa for Iran, he will pay for her trip and services as a translator. Robert has the idea that once we invade Iraq, journalists can slip across the border from Iran and move about much more freely than those embedded with the armed forces. I tell Robert I'll go, too. I want to see this war close-up.

I believe in the war; I think we should remove Saddam. I don't know if Iraq has weapons of mass destruction; in fact, I doubt it. Like the Soviet Union in its last days, Iraq is too misman-aged and impoverished to be a military threat to the United States. But Saddam is an evil man who regularly slaughters his own people, and as a Jew, I feel that if I'm not willing to support American intervention to save innocent people, I have no right to complain that the world stood by as the Nazis slaughtered the Jews. *It's the right war for the wrong reason,* I told Amir, and he agreed.

But I've also been fascinated with war itself as long as I can re-call. I've always felt that war, terrible as it is, reveals truths that are accessible no other way. Since even now women don't see combat in the American armed forces, I feel excluded or spared, and ashamed of that feeling.

As a freelance writer with no war experience, I have little chance of being chosen to be embedded. Robert's plan might just work, and I figure I'll have half a leg up speaking some Farsi. The only problem is that Shirin refuses point-blank to help me get an Iranian visa. As a Jew, she says, I'll be in too much danger. If anything goes wrong, the Iranian government could charge me with spying for Israel.

When I told Amir that I wanted to go to Iraq, he said, *I don't understand the way Americans are curious about war.* I couldn't tell if he wanted me to go or not. And if he didn't, was it because he would miss me or because he wanted to be the one to leave first? This gets at my other and worse reason to go to Iraq: to escape what's happening, or not happening, with Amir. The last night we were together, it was bliss as always. But after the brunch I finally took him to, and a trip to a sporting goods store where Amir bought winter boots for Afghanistan, he didn't phone me. He's stopped calling; he only e-mails.

I walk into the bar, one of the self-consciously upscale lounges that have proliferated in Manhattan recently. It's filled with people who look like the friends of Amir I've already met: thirtysomething, Ivy League, bourgeois. And there at a banquette in the back is Amir, sitting with three plump men in blue blazers.

When Amir sees me, he looks dazed, as though he can't quite remember who I am. I realize from his body language that he's had a lot to drink, and it's not even eleven.

"*Ann jan!*" he finally calls out, and I say hello, but I remain still, waiting for him to stand to greet me. Finally he remembers his manners and rises tentatively to his feet, unsure of his coordination. He walks over and kisses me on the cheek, then excuses himself. I talk with a few of his friends, and then Shirin comes in and we chat. It's been nearly a half hour and Amir hasn't returned.

A work colleague of his is asking me why I decided to learn Farsi, and while I'm starting to explain, I hear Amir's voice, sneering. "Yes, Ann, why *are* you learning Farsi?"

I have the sense that it offends him, and this infuriates me. I restrain the impulse to ask him whether he owns the Persian language; I remember just in time that Amir has told me he prefers speaking English to Farsi because Farsi is "a muddy language." He might not understand why a foreigner would bother. And I answer truthfully that I'm learning Persian because I fell in love with Afghanistan.

A dozen times I want to leave, and I wonder if Amir will leave without me or create a scene as he did on our second night together. But Amir stays just this side of rude. As the bar closes, he and I and Don walk out together and head downtown, toward Don's house and mine. When we reach Don's building, Amir pleads with him: "I'm exhausted—can I crash on your couch?" If he does that, I'll never talk to him again. But Don says he can't. And as Amir and I continue walking south, I see a tear fall from his eye. I reach up to wipe it away, and he relaxes, his mood changes instantly, and we are together again. I can't even find it in me to be angry with him anymore.

I spent my twenties and thirties bursting into rages, some deserved, with my boyfriends. If I was able to avoid that with Amir, was it because I'd become more mature, or—I was afraid—because he seemed so defenseless?

Inside my house, Amir asks for a margarita. I try to start a fire in my sitting-room fireplace, but it burns poorly. I don't try too hard, since I expect him to kiss me, but instead he begins to talk.

Last week I thought of you once when I wasn't supposed to.

Just once?

I've been very depressed. Sometimes I have trouble getting myself to go to work.

Depressed? Amir's e-mails of the last two weeks have been obnoxiously full of reasons why he is too busy to see me. There was the Princeton squash fund-raiser and the eating-club dinner and drinks with work colleagues, birthday parties, and birthday dinners. Although he's come to my friends' parties and mine, he never invites me to anything.

I can't believe I'm still here. I've wanted to go to Afghanistan ever since 9/11, and I still don't have a green card!

I'm sorry, but I can't help you with that one, you know. *Amir jan,* I'm glad you haven't gone. You're so amazing in bed—do you know that no one has ever made love to me so many times?

Amir says quietly, Did I ever mention that I've never had anything like this, either?

No, you were too macho to say you're wonderful.

It's not me, it's us.

Then I feel crude for what I said and for what I didn't say: that I adore him and haven't ever felt so much for a man's body, that I can't believe I'll have to do without him soon. Fear keeps me quiet: His mood could turn in an instant to the coldness of the first part of the evening. And nothing in the way he's treated me lately makes me want to tell him that I care for him.

We go upstairs, and I change the sheets so he won't be bothered by the cat hair. You treat me like a prince, he says, surprised, and I reply proudly, Why shouldn't I?

Long past dawn, we've finished making love yet again, and I realize my eyes are wet. He wipes my tears away. It's not only the first time I've cried in front of him—it's the first time I've cried in front of a man for many years. There hasn't been anyone I trusted not to walk away.

I stop pretending to sleep before Amir does, and go down to the sitting room to retrieve my clothes. His jeans are also lying on the floor where he pulled them off in haste, and his wallet is half out of the back pocket. I listen to make sure he's not coming down the stairs. And, crouching on the floor, I lift the wallet out of his pants, being careful to remember which side was up. The black leather feels much cheaper than I would have imagined; it's cracked with age rather than grown burnished and supple, as fine leather does. It's not what I'd expect from a Princeton grad at his firm, but leather connoisseurship probably isn't a big thing among Afghans. Inside, there's almost nothing. I don't know exactly what I'm looking for—another woman's number?—but it's not there. There's just a credit card, his work ID, some twenties. Not even a driver's license.

Reaching into an inside compartment, my fingers close on a card. I pull it out. It's mine, now grimy and dog-eared, the one I gave Amir when I first invited him over in October.

I have to sit down for a moment then, and as I hold my head in my hands, tears come to my eyes. I no longer know which is worse: the idea that he might care for me as much as I care for him—and still act this way—or the idea that he doesn't care. And then, on no sleep, I go to my Saturday morning Farsi class.

When I come back, Amir is up and hungry. I make eggs and chicken sausage and pierogi, a Jewish breakfast with fake pork, I joke. I've never had sausage before, Amir admits, and I wonder how he's managed that.

If I were with that girl from your Farsi class—what was her name?

Fruzan.

She's a Pashtun like him, tall and lovely and twenty years younger than me; I introduced her to Amir when we ran into her once. Amir and I were still only friends then, but I was secretly pleased that he didn't seem interested. He said Fruzan was too dark for him.

If I were with Fruzan now, she would take care of me.

Unlike me?

He is silent, and then says, very quietly, No.

He's not talking about cooking. Just last night he told me that I treated him like a prince. At face value this remark is about my not being an Afghan; an Afghan woman would make him feel more cared for. Or maybe not—maybe if he were with Fruzan, he'd be tormenting her by saying, "If I were with an American." Maybe it's got nothing to do with nationalities, just with Amir's wish to hurt anyone who loves him.

I'm wounded enough to raise a subject that's been bothering me: When I found out you don't talk to your younger brother, I gave up hope for you.

I know this is none of my business. I'd be outraged if Amir told me how he thought I ought to treat my family. But I feel I have to mention it. There really is no hope for us if his mind rules his heart. This used to be something I admired. It was how I thought of myself at one stage. But now I think it's a terrible thing. Amir has a big and passionate heart that he's done his best to shrink and stifle. He couldn't talk so poignantly of his "lost" brother if he didn't know what it meant to love him. The terrible part is that knowing the price of his loyalty to tradition, he will go ahead and pay it anyway. If he can turn away from the little brother he used to carry on his shoulders, he can turn away from me, and I can never trust him, and this is doomed.

I'm bracing for him to stand up from the table and say he has to go, but instead it feels as if the ice has broken. He smiles and says something completely unexpected: One of the philosophers I studied at Princeton wrote that hope must be created.

I can hardly believe my ears. It's like finding my business card in Amir's wallet when I looked for evidence of duplicity. Only the man of my dreams would say what Amir just said. It's elegant and reassuring, and seems to come from a man who's older and wiser than I am.

But I remember too well how he treated me last night. I need to speak my mind, and I continue. I have a bad temper, you know. If I haven't shown it, it's not because I don't get angry. When you treat me like a stranger, the way you did at the party last night—you were so rude—

I'm sorry, I didn't mean to hurt you. And then he says, There will be plenty of time for you to show me your bad temper next year when I get back from Afghanistan.

I can't quite believe what I've heard—it's like the remark about loving me that slipped by me our first night, and it might be the nicest thing a man has said to me in years. It gives me the courage to probe further.

If you're so worried about getting your green card so you can go to Afghanistan, why don't you just marry your friend Ellen?

I might go anyway, even without the green card.

Amir has mentioned this before. When I told Luisa, who'd recently got her own green card, she said no one in his right mind would take that risk: *They might not let him back into the United States, and then he'd have to stay in Afghanistan. And he'll never do that. He likes his American comforts too well, and the drinking, and the parties.*

I'm thinking of this, but I say something different. Amir, I know you want to marry an Afghan. And I know you don't want a child now; I didn't either at your age. But I just want you to remember, if your immigration situation doesn't work out, I'll marry you so you can get a green card if you get me pregnant.

I expect him to be horrified, but he still looks happy and relaxed. He just says, Thank you for your offer. I'm going to deal with the marriage issue after I get back from Afghanistan. And that's all we say about what's going on between us.

Later that afternoon I read aloud to Amir from one of my favorite essays.

> The psychopath is notoriously difficult to analyze because
> the fundamental decision of his nature is to try to live the
> infantile fantasy, and in this decision (given the dreary al-
> ternative of psychoanalysis) there may be a certain instinc-
> tive wisdom . . . If one is to change one's habits, one must
> go back to the source of their creation, and so the psy-
> chopath exploring backward along the road of the homo-
> sexual, the orgiast, the drug-addict, the rapist, the robber
> and the murderer seeks to find those violent parallels to the
> violent and often hopeless contradictions he knew as an in-
> fant and as a child. For if he has the courage to meet the
> parallel situation at the moment when he is ready, then he
> has a chance to act as he has never acted before, and in sat-
> isfying the frustration . . . may then pass by symbolic substi-
> tute through the locks of incest.

This reading aloud is a strange, nerdy thing to do, but I mean
it as passionately as I know how. The passage is from Norman
Mailer's essay "The White Negro." Published in 1957, a year
before I was born, and now more known for its title than its
contents, it was meant as an explanation of the hipster in
American society. Amir didn't grow up in the shadow of the
Beats, and he doesn't care about many of the issues that ob-
sess Mailer; unlike Mailer and unlike me, he has no experience
of psychoanalysis. But I think Amir might be interested in
what Mailer says about reinventing oneself. After all, it's what
he's had to do since he got to this country. And he seems to
know that something is wrong with him, just as I know something is wrong with me. And Amir is quiet—receptive, it could
be, or maybe just exhausted. But it seems as we sit together in

the still, cold afternoon that we might yet save each other, that we might be able to defy both our individual and our con-joined doom.

That night, after we go out to see a movie whose title is oddly apropos—*Catch Me If You Can*—Amir speaks again of a future in which we are together. Maybe we can go to a warm place next winter, when I come back from Afghanistan. He stashes some cigarettes in my kitchen drawer and asks if I can wash a pair of his socks that got wet. As he leaves he says, I'll come by in a few days and give you another Dari lesson. And I'm as happy as I've ever been with him.

March 19, 2003, is the night we begin our war against Saddam Hussein and it's also my brother's thirty-ninth birthday. He's arranged a dinner for ten at Le Cirque, but the mood is far from festive. The grand dining room is as deserted as if it were in Baghdad itself. Voices are low at our table and the atmosphere is subdued, though most of us support the invasion.

I walk the two miles home, thinking of the war. Three of my friends are over there now—Dina in Iraqi Kurdistan, Jason embedded with an army unit in Kuwait for his newspaper, and Robert (who's given up on Iran) in Jordan. I wonder if I should have tried harder to go myself. It would be better than watching it on TV and waiting to hear from Amir.

It's been ten days since Amir said he would come by for a Dari lesson, and it's just a couple of days before Norouz when he said he'd be back in Afghanistan. I called him a few days after we saw the movie—the first time I'd phoned in a couple of weeks. I got his voice mail and said hello.

The next day he sent me an e-mail: *Sorry I was out with some guys from the office when you called. Let's get together this weekend for some Afghan cooking and a movie, if I don't have to travel on business.*

This sounded encouraging, and I replied, *That would be great, but I find it so depressing when I get an e-mail in reply to a phone call. Can we please talk on the phone?*

His response was immediate: *Please excuse my telephobia, but remember that I didn't grow up talking on the phone with my girlfriends after school. I prefer to talk with a woman in person, when I can hold her and look into her eyes. But I hope you will understand that I am very busy now, I am trying to get packed and ready to go.*

And this polite and even tender e-mail makes me burst into tears. So I've fallen into the trap after all. My mild request that we talk on the phone got Amir talking about packing to go to Afghanistan. Why does the phone scare him so? His comment about not talking to his girlfriends on the phone after school is a non sequitur; while he didn't grow up using the phone regularly the way Americans do, he didn't grow up with e-mail at all. I remember the *New Yorker* cartoon where two dogs are chatting, and one says, "on the Internet, no one knows you're a dog." On the Internet, if you write English well enough, no one knows you're not a native English speaker. On the phone, though, Amir can't efface the accent that comes with having learned English so late.

I love Amir's sonorous, rich voice, manly but with a tiny hint of affectation and snobbery. I find it charming and full of flavor; I enjoy his foreign accent, as I do those of so many of my other friends born overseas. But does this accent mean to him what it means to me? Perhaps he feels about his accent as my mother did about a Jewish accent: she made sure not to have one. I've been told I have a "Harvard accent," but my mother—her first language Yiddish, NYU class of '48—sounds more upper-class than I do.

It might have been that the voice means not too little to Amir but too much. His telephobia is selective. When we were together at my house on the weekends and he went out to buy groceries or cigarettes, he sometimes called twice in fifteen minutes, asking directions, or what type of tomatoes to buy, or whether I had peanut oil. It was as if he couldn't bear to be out of touch for even so short a time, once he was in the mood. And in that mood, when he was open to intimacy and love, he wanted to hear my voice and to let me hear his.

But when we were apart during the workweek and he e-mailed me, he could act as if we were just casual buddies. Online he seemed to want to slowly push me away until one of us disappeared into the Middle East, beyond the reach of all but satellite phones. Although a stranger would not see anything in his last e-mail to prove it, I somehow know it's over. My Sheherezad game has failed. My body knows I won't see him again. That's why I weep the moment I read his e-mail.

I smoke the cigarettes Amir had stashed in my kitchen. That little gesture toward a future visit now looks like an inversion of the American cliché of the man who goes out for cigarettes and never comes back. Maybe he left them there in a futile effort to fight his impulse to do just that. It reminds me of the movie we saw that last night, *Catch Me If You Can,* whose con man antihero was always walking out of the lives of smitten women one step ahead of disclosure. I throw away the socks Amir left. They're so worn he really should have done the same. I hide the huge rolled-up map of Afghanistan he gave me at the back of a library shelf, where I won't have to look at it except when I'm following the news; I'm too practical to throw out such a good map. The only other things he's left behind are cooking supplies, which break my heart to consider.

I wonder if it's something I said the last time we were together, if he had a delayed panic when my offer to marry him if he gave me a baby sank in. But I don't think it really did. I don't think Amir feels the same way about words as I do. He doesn't think I really meant it, any more than he really meant it when he envisioned a future where I showed him my bad temper. We never played by the usual rules anyway; most men don't talk to the women they're seeing about their plans for an arranged marriage.

My friends tell me, *He's just another jerk*, *What do you want with a guy who won't make a commitment*, *He's too immature*. Luisa says, "He has a lot of growing up to do before he becomes a real person," and there's none of the usual amusement in her voice, just sadness. Jason points out that except for the fact that Amir can bear not to see me, I have more power than Amir does. I'm richer, better connected, better educated, older, more confident. The only thing Amir has is the power of his refusal. This interests me. But what man gives up making love a dozen times a night simply to enjoy the power of refusal?

Rebecca pulls at her long red hair and cautions, "There is too much repression there." And Samuel thinks he knows precisely what the problem is: "Amir can't both fuck and talk to a woman. That's why he won't call you. I know that sex is important to you, and Amir is a very good lover. But forget about him. Sex isn't everything. He's a pain in the ass."

I take what Samuel says seriously, even though he's never met Amir. Samuel is the only friend I have who's actually done what Amir claims to want to do. After he finished grad school in the United States, he went back to Colombia and married his second cousin Rebecca. Out of love, it's true, but Rebecca told me that just after she was born, her father turned to Samuel's father, his cousin, and said, "Someday your son will marry my daughter." Colombian Jews, Rebecca explained, rarely marry out of the faith; I joked that they rarely even married out of the family.

If Samuel is right, Amir wouldn't be able to be candid with a woman he saw mainly in sexual terms. Perhaps he really did need an Afghan bride, who was, as he said to Luisa in the fall, for the kitchen. Maybe he wanted an arranged marriage, not in spite of its potential sexual torpor but because of it. When Amir confessed, *I've never had anything like this* on our last night together, I assumed that was a reason for us to see each other. But it looks as if I was dead wrong.

As the war continues, I wake hours too early, forget to eat, and check my e-mail constantly for the message from Amir that doesn't arrive. I think I'll watch the war on TV and I keep it on, sound off, most of the day, but I can't look at it often.

Consciously, the bombing doesn't bother me much, nor do the deaths of Saddam's troops—at least the ones who want to fight. I believe (and later, when I go to Baghdad in May, will learn for a fact) that civilian deaths are being kept to a minimum, that the bombing is indeed surgically precise, and that we're acting in the best interests of the Iraqi people. And every time I read reportage on the war in the paper or a magazine, I wonder if I could have done better, and I miss my chance to have tried. I wish I were there. But unconsciously, the war is immensely depressing. What I see on TV mingles with my feelings of loss over Amir, feelings that are visceral before anything else. I feel as though I've been hit by a truck anyway, and I feel even worse every time I look at the TV.

I wonder how Amir feels. Shirin called him at work the day after the bombing began, but he wasn't in; his secretary said he'd called in sick. He'd supported the war, but maybe he was depressed about the bombs falling on his fellow Muslims—*my brothers,* he had called them when describing waiting in line to register at the INS. He was my only friend who actually fought in a war. Was the buildup to the war bringing back bad memories? When he last talked about bringing me some of his books, one of the titles he mentioned was Clausewitz's *On War.*

I might have probed more into Amir's *mujahid* days if I'd thought differently about war, but on some level for me, war would always be the Allies in World War II, heroic and straightforward. My father and my uncles had been decorated combat veterans, and like many other Jewish vets, they felt a personal satisfaction in defeating Nazi Germany. I grew up on my dad's war stories, and while he told of his fear in battle and hinted at terrible sights, my overall impression was of excitement and drama combined with feats of endurance I measured myself against. He carried a submachine gun and a pack that weighed only thirty pounds less than he did; he won a

Bronze Star for being in one of the first boats to cross the Rhine into Germany.

My dad might have censored a great deal when he spoke to us children, but when he enlisted after high school graduation in 1944 he hadn't even turned eighteen, the same age Amir had been when he'd fought the Soviets. My father had seen with a child's eyes. In his letters home he asks for sweets and, even when describing what must have been harrowing experiences, he maintains a casual tone:

> We crossed under quite severe fire with what was called by the papers "light opposition." I was in the first wave and our section was attached to the leading rifle troops. From that morning on until that evening when we got tank support we were in what seemed to be a nightmare. Several men in our section were hit and one was almost killed in the resulting 20mm and burp-gun fire. The section that consisted of about 15 men was all within a small area when those men were hit. That was one time when I never thought I'd see the next day. But again I was fooled and the remaining two days of the attack passed without much happening. It was then that we started going twenty or thirty miles a day chasing the Germans.

My father got the Bronze Star for what the press called "crossing under light opposition." He was not yet twenty.

His war was a short one. He came down with rheumatic fever in the last days of the European theater, spent a year in army hospitals, and returned home to resume college. But sometime after my father came home he also took his teenage younger sister to bed.

Most therapies for war trauma, from Freud's work with shell-shocked World War I veterans to today's behavioral treatments, recommend getting the sufferer to talk about his experiences as a way of exorcising them, and this might have been what my father was doing in his stories to us children. Amir told me no war stories. But then, it was totally outside the Pashtun cultural tradition to admit to any response to danger other than contemptuous bravery.

Amir's war experience was part of his glamour for me, one of the manly virtues I admired him for, distinguishing him from the soft, unmartial American men of my generation and background. Sometimes he talked as if he felt that way, too. But I was wondering now if it had ruined something in him, wondering, too, if my father's war had ruined something in him, shattered whatever usually keeps a man from making love to his younger sister.

There's something strikingly un-American about brother-sister incest; it reeks of the darker corners of the Old World, of the ancient Near Eastern tradition of cousin marriage that was part of the Jewish not-so-distant past, as it is of the Afghan present. In many Arab tribes, Germaine Tillion points out, the word for "female cousin" is the same as the word for "sister." The North African language of love itself recognizes the practice of marrying the almost-sister: "In both Arabic-speaking countries and areas of the Berber language a poet calls the woman he loves 'my sister.' When the author of the love-song is a woman, she calls her lover 'my brother.'"

The famous jealousy of men in Mediterranean and Muslim societies regarding their sisters' honor is to some degree a displacement of sexual desire. Of course men in these societies are supposed to defend their sisters' virginity against all but family-approved suitors, not to take it themselves, but it is clearly a temptation in any family structure that marries men to the women most closely related to them after their sisters.

My father's war might have led in a direct line to my falling in love with Amir. More and more I thought that Amir's statement that he wanted an arranged marriage had sharpened my interest in him. Although I didn't know about my father's incest until my mother told me in my midtwenties, the knowledge was in the ambience of my childhood. It might have been what kept my brother and me so physically reserved with each other—even now we hardly kiss on greeting. And combined with the tense and sad atmosphere of my childhood, it made me eager to separate sex from domesticity, to remove making love from keeping house. It was why I loved sex with strangers. It was why I wanted a man who looked Jewish but wasn't; one who looked like family but couldn't be.

When I thought as a child that married couples had to have similar first names, I might have been responding to the unlikeliness of any other reason for my parents to be together. But it is possible that I knew something about love and relatedness and having a name in common that I could not put into words. I thought I could marry only a relative, even while knowing that such marriages are forbidden. And with Amir, who resembled my father's father, Harry, down to his hooked nose and thick black hair, I had gone my unconscious one better. The engines of my family's peculiar craziness fired up when I met a man who wouldn't marry me because I wasn't his relative.

When Amir disappeared in mid-March, I cried only once, alone, reading his e-mail about packing. I've never been one for tears—so much so, that when I told a male friend to read a book because it made me weep, he was impressed: "If it made *you* cry . . ." I think of myself as tenderhearted, but others may not.

It takes a month for the tears to come again, this time very awkwardly, in front of several people at Samuel and Rebecca's house. Samuel is horsing around with me and takes my bare foot into his huge mouth for a moment. Then he laughs, "How small your toes are!" And I remember how Amir spoke of my *baby feet*, and for the first time since childhood, I burst into tears in public. They scatter great distances, and I'm mortified.

I still half agree with Luisa, sitting close by, who said, "Treat him like your boy toy and you'll be fine." She and my other friends are eager to tell me how immature and disturbed and cruel Amir is, and to urge me to forget about him. Their intentions are the best, and in the past I counseled them in the same tones when they spoke longingly of boyfriends I thought were bad for them. But I realize that something in me has changed. I can't see Amir as my *boy toy*. Even the language is loathsome to me. Hot tears spill down my face. I'm ashamed of how lightly I used to take love and angry that it's the norm in my culture.

At a party in mid-April I told the story of Amir's disappearance to a pyschologist friend. He crisply offered his advice: "He won't commit to you. Forget about him and move on." I wondered just what store of cultural wisdom this drew upon, even as I winced at the *commit*. Would the world have had much of its store of love poetry had earlier cultures thought like this? Does it matter whether I love Amir, or he me? Apparently not. Are these feelings worth honoring, even in their failure? Apparently not. Just how long am I entitled to be sad before hastening to the online personals and searching for a forty-five-year-old Jewish professional who likes long walks and good restaurants?

Afghans were not ashamed to cry over lost loves, I knew, but I didn't need to go so far afield for a counterexample. In earlier times in the West, tears were a woman's privilege and respected as a sign of serious emotion. But now weeping over a man is considered an error of judgment. Tears suggest that the person shedding them has made the gravest miscalculation of all, giving more than one receives. Deep grief is the sign of a bad bargain, and nothing is worse in a commercial culture. Americans are notoriously averse to mourning death, but we're no better with lost love.

When Rebecca asks, "What's happened to you? I thought of

you as so independent and strong," I realize that I no longer think of strength the way she means. I'm sick of listening to friends, however beloved, tell me how they admire me for being strong, or how women should be strong, or that the problem with men is that they can't stand strong women. What's now meant by strength is the ability to conceal and re-press any susceptibility to the charm of another person, any tenderness not precisely paid for by appropriate behavior, any kindness that might be unreciprocated—indeed, love itself, ex-cept when duly justified by a legal bond and a mortgage. In other words, strength means callousness, and I've been good at that. But now I no longer believe that strength means tak-ing love casually. And I start to think that the main problem with men and women in our culture is that all of us are afraid of feeling and especially of feeling grief.

My tears are as natural a response to Amir's absence as mak-ing love had been to his presence. The tears elude judgment and opinion; they come whether I want them to or not, whether I want him back more than anything in the world or wish him dead, as I alternately do. Sometimes I worry that I'm growing addicted to melancholy. But I'm sad, not depressed, and it's right that I should be sad. And gradually I come to welcome rather than dread my tears, for in those moments my body and heart are one, as they were when I was in bed with Amir.

And so I feel justified when I cry over Amir—not every day but a few times a week, sometimes just for a minute but sometimes hours at a time, while reading, while trying to sleep, while sit-ting in the sun, while driving. Tears stream from my eyes so abundantly that I find myself wondering how I'm producing these ounces of water. Even when Scott left me after seven years for the woman he eventually married, I didn't weep like this. The change has as much to do with me as with the man who caused my tears. I've become able to admit, and even to value, feelings in myself that I would once have called weakness.

I may have been more receptive to Amir when I returned from my second trip to Afghanistan, not just because I thought well of Afghans but because my experiences there made me able to appreciate qualities in Amir that I wasn't able to name or consciously acknowledge. Though when Amir and I were friends, I told people that he fought for his country as a teenager and seemed physically fearless, I must have sensed the damage that gave him trouble sleeping decades after his war experience and that made him fear dying a violent death if he returned to his country. But every time Amir allowed me to see this more vulnerable side—and he usually had to be cruel to me first, maybe to justify the rejection he sensed coming or to invite it as punishment for his disclosure—I denied it. It frightened me. The idea that he could be weak frightened me.

After three weeks of silence I decide I have little to lose by e-mailing Amir. I'm cautious and prosaic, suggesting that we should talk, and that if he wants, we could be friends rather than lovers. I hope he won't pick that option, and he doesn't; he doesn't reply at all. My e-mail seems ugly to me. So a few days later I try again, writing, *I know your body by heart—or is it the other way around?—and I won't forget you.*

A day later, Amir replies, *I thought you might have given up on me by now. I feel terrible about falling out of touch with you. This hasn't been a good time for me. I can't believe it's after Norouz and I'm not in Afghanistan. I'm still trying to get the damn green card so I can get the hell out of here. I promise to see you before I go.*

I want to write, *See me before you go? You said you'd see me in a few days, and that was a month ago*—but I don't want to play that part. Even if I never see Amir again, I decide I won't be the American woman who demands but does not give. But I have no idea what to reply to *I thought you might have given up on me by now.* How sad if he really thought that after just a few weeks. It would be even worse if he thought I was over him because he was over me. Part of me wants to write Amir a passionate letter telling him that I won't give up on him now or ever, that I want him, that I need to see him.

But then I think. As Luisa pointed out, it could take Amir months to get his green card, and he'd be reckless to leave without it. Seeing me before he leaves might mean next year, and saying so might be an especially cowardly way of putting me off. I remember Sarah's now-prescient-sounding e-mail about Afghan men: *They have all ultimately behaved like cads to the Western women they've been involved with.*

I weigh the person suggested by Amir's e-mail against the man Amir was in my house, a man who made me feel adored, who showed me his fears and his tears and never spoke a word of criticism to me, the one who told me just a few weeks ago, *Hope must be created.* For a different woman the e-mail might have sunk in the balance against how I felt when I was with Amir. But I'm hurt and angry, and I've had too many bad experiences with men. And I'm a writer—I take a person's written words seriously. Amir's words are banal, cold, evasive. I write nothing at all.

A few weeks later, a few weeks of sleeplessness and misery, I ask Shirin to sound Amir out about me. He has no trouble returning her call immediately or answering her faux-casual question about whether he's seen me lately. She reports back to me that he said point-blank, "I'm avoiding Ann. Things were getting very intense. I don't want to have a serious relationship with her; I'm going to Afghanistan. It's not her fault, she never put any pressure on me; in fact, she's being so mature about how I am avoiding her—she's great."

I'm crushed by the banality of his language, the *intense* and *serious relationship* and *so mature*—ugly American talk from someone who knows hundreds of lines of Rumi and Hafez, someone who allowed me to hear *making love* as something other than a euphemism. Amir seemed outside what I considered callous American ways of thinking about love and sex. I thought he was part of that other world where fifty years was not enough. When we were together I often felt that his emotions were purer than mine, no matter how confused and poorly modulated. I tried to rise to what I thought of as their level, but I was too frightened of Amir leaving me to open my heart to him anywhere but in bed. And now he spoke as though he did not know what he had taught me.

"I think he'll see you again—it sounded that way, but I don't know why you'd bother," Shirin says. "He's not worth it. He doesn't even talk to his younger brother. He's not very noble. He's a confused guy from Afghanistan sitting in a filthy little apartment in Brooklyn."

A terrible possibility occurs to me: Maybe Amir never allowed me to see his apartment not so much because it was small and filthy but because, in his culture, having me as a guest would have magnified my claims on him a hundredfold. A Pashtun must do everything a guest asks, even defend him to the death. It did not seem that the guest has reciprocal obligations. My stomach turns over as I wonder if Amir avoided becoming my host to make sure he could someday betray my trust. I wait for him to send me an e-mail explaining what he said to Shirin, but it never comes.

The war is drawing to a close as I hang on Amir's e-mail, and I feel ashamed of being so preoccupied with a lover as a dictatorship falls. I'm proud of Jason and Dina as I read their dispatches and sorry that I'm not there with them. Part of me feels that it would have been the test of my courage and acuity and empathy, and I mean it when I tell incredulous friends, "I would rather be at the front lines than going through this nightmare with Amir." I hate uncertainty more than danger, and hate nothing more than waiting. But part of me also knows that for these very reasons what I'm going through with Amir—nightmarish, silly, childish, tragic, whatever description I put on it, which changes from day to day—is just as much a test of who I am and who I could be as going to the war would have been.

Toward the end of April, a couple of weeks after Baghdad falls, I send Amir an article I've published, and he responds with a few polite lines, just a bit more personal than a form letter. I answer in kind, and I pride myself on keeping my end short and sweet, telling Amir that I miss him but never reproaching him. We exchange e-mail every few days for a couple of weeks,

but his are short and flavorless, and I have to remind myself
that he isn't a native speaker, and on top of that he's an engineer, not a writer. In person, Amir is capable of laconic wit and
the occasional graceful phrase, of charm and warmth. But
maybe that's what he's afraid of showing me now. And I grow
silently angrier by the day at his refusal to talk with me on the
phone, angry not just at the coldness it shows but at the way
he is forcing me to lower my opinion of him.

Then one day he sends me a warmer e-mail, ending, *You've been
in my thoughts; let's get together soon.* I suggest that he meet Shirin
and me for a drink after our Farsi lesson in a few days. I tell
him that we don't have to have any kind of probing discussion of what's happening between us. It's just a friendly get-
together. Having Shirin there will reassure him, I hope. I
assume that once we see each other, Amir will remember how
he feels about me, and we will be in touch again. And my strategy seems to work. Amir e-mails that he'll come by if he doesn't
have to work late; he'll call me later. That afternoon the phone
rings, and the caller ID shows Amir's cell phone number. But
when I say hello, trying to modulate my excitement—it's late
April now and the first time he's called me since late February—I hear a business conversation in the background. Amir
obviously hit the speed dial buttons for my number by acci-
dent. I'm furious: he's so adamant about not talking to me on
the phone, yet he still has my number programmed? This mis-
chance seems more churlish than his silence.

When he never calls or comes over that night, I give up at last.
It's time to leave town and forget about this. Rebecca has invited me to visit her and Samuel in Bogotá for her thirty-fifth
birthday party in late June, and I buy a ticket. Then I e-mail

Dina, who's in Baghdad now, and tell her I'm thinking of coming to Iraq in mid-May and staying until it's time to go to Colombia. I want to see what's happening, and it's exciting that Ahmed Chalabi is being spoken of as a possible future head of state. I met him a couple of times in New York through Dina, who's an old friend; she and her boyfriend once brought him to a small gathering at my house. Maybe I could write something interesting about him. Dina answers that it's easy to get to Baghdad now—you just take a cab from Amman. *Come soon; it's getting very hot. Bring a bathing suit. There's a great pool at my hotel. I have to leave soon, but if you don't get here while I'm around we can meet up in Amman.*

Then I craft a final e-mail to Amir expressing all of my anger, though none of my pain. I don't mention my tears or my longing, just how badly he's treating me. *Why don't you have any respect for my time or my feelings? If you can tell Shirin what's going on why can't you tell me? I would never treat a lover like this,* I write, and it's true. I have a bad temper, but I'm direct, and I don't avoid hard conversations if they're the right thing to do. *Do you ever think about how you would feel in my shoes? Don't you have any notion that you should do unto others as you would have them do unto you? Would you respect a woman who treated you as you're treating me? Show me that you're not as cowardly and selfish as you seem.*

I don't send the e-mail. I still have a tiny bit of hope that he might pick up the phone and be what I used to think of as himself again. What's happened to the grave and earnest young man I came to know over the fall? To the vulnerable and sad one who told me to hope? Even the angry man who said he couldn't be my boyfriend spoke with a rough decency I no longer sense.

And then, a few days later, I run into Amir. It's a cool May evening and I'm going to meet my friend Alexandra at a screening of a documentary about Afghanistan made by a friend of hers. I'm playing tennis afterward, so I show up wearing running pants and sneakers and a sweatshirt, a choice I instantly regret when I see Amir.

It takes me a moment to recognize the man getting out of the cab just in front of me. Amir looks relaxed and happy and well-groomed, fresh from work, the way I remember him from the fall, but also impenetrable and ordinary, another preppy guy in a suit and tie. In the winter Amir looked vulnerable and soulful, with unshaven cheeks and eyes shadowed from lack of sleep. Those images are still fresh to me: I've pored over the handful of photos I took of him until I know them by heart: Amir in the knee-high snow in front of my house; Amir smoking in the winter dawn; Amir sprawled on the easy chair in my living room, jocular and flirtatious; Amir grave and wan, lost in his thoughts. In one of those photos, Amir is wearing the same blue and white striped shirt he has on tonight, but the openness and defenselessness I recall from the photos are missing in the jolly ex–frat boy standing at the curb.

Amir smiles broadly when he sees me and kisses me on the cheek. Are you going to the movie? I thought you might go to this one.

I also thought there was a slight chance Amir would come to the movie, since it's one of the few about his country, but I figured that this showing was too early for him, that he'd still be at the office. I guessed wrong. And instead of feeling the rush of joy I've imagined at seeing Amir again after two months,

I feel rage. After the energy I've spent thinking about him and trying to get him to see me, after the hours I've spent crying over his loss, to run into him by chance is worse than not seeing him at all.

I can't control the anger in my voice. Well, why didn't you call me then? Weren't we supposed to get together last week? I continue grimly: Look Amir, we're both here, why don't we just get a coffee and chat for fifteen minutes?

I can't, I'm meeting a friend. But how about after the movie?

I agree. And I walk away to give him some privacy. When I turn around, a block away, I can see Amir standing on the sidewalk, staring at me. I turn my back and walk farther away, hardly able to breathe.

Alexandra and I stand outside the theater just before the film begins, and Amir walks up to us. He's with a very short, very plain girl, blond, and I'm relieved; surely the man who made a fuss about tall women isn't dating someone barely five feet tall. I introduce Alexandra and Amir introduces his friend, and then we all walk in. I can hardly concentrate on the screening. I'm running different scenarios in my mind for my talk with Amir, who is sitting ten rows ahead of me. He doesn't turn around. Afterward, I wait in the lobby with Alexandra. Suddenly I hear a familiar voice. It's Rebecca, here by coincidence for a South American film playing after the one I've just seen. As I'm telling her Amir is here, he walks by us. He looks neither to the left nor to the right as he moves toward the exit, trailed by the short girl. When I call his name, he turns and gives a wooden half wave, still walking away.

I go after him. Amir, you said we could talk after the movie!

Can't, have to go to dinner with friends. And he continues walking.

Amir! I try again, in a low voice full of such fury that it stops him in his tracks. I need to talk to you right now.

And finally he follows me to a place on the sidewalk away from our friends. I can't believe this is the same man I once thought brave and good. I want to shout at him, but I don't want to create a public scene. I keep my voice controlled, but he must hear the rage underneath.

Listen, when we first started seeing each other, you promised me you would always treat me with respect. You're not doing that now.

I am treating you with respect.

No, you're not.

I don't want to have this conversation now.

Well, when are we going to have it? I've been trying to see you for two months.

I've been busy; it hasn't worked out.

Busy for two months? Listen Amir, I'm not asking you as a girlfriend or even as a friend—but just as a human being—to treat me as you would wish to be treated. I haven't been able to sleep for two months because of this. His eyes narrow with an expression I recognize as pleasure, the same pleasure I gave him in bed.

Let's get this over with, Amir. I'm traveling soon—

So am I.

And I just want to finish this.

I'll e-mail you.

No! I *never* want to get another e-mail from you. You can call me!

Okay, I'll call you. Now I've got to go.

When I get home after tennis, I stay up till dawn, polishing the scathing e-mail I'd begun and never sent. I'm still hoping Amir will keep his word and call me, but he doesn't. I didn't think I could feel worse than during Amir's disappearance, but now I do—for then I felt the loss of love and sex bitterly but still had the consolation of wholehearted longing for him. Now I don't have that, either. When he tried to sneak out of the movie theater without talking with me, he forfeited every last bit of my respect and admiration. I still desire him, but I despise him now, too, and I weep and weep. Two days after the movie screening, I send the e-mail.

part three

The one who enters between
the onion and its skin receives
nothing except a bad odor.

—Iraqi proverb

We kiss for the first time the moment I close the front door to my house, and it's thrilling. Soon Kemal is reaching down to pull my thin black tank top off, and I congratulate myself on my good luck: finally a one-night stand that might blur my muscle memory of Amir. It's been two and a half weeks since I ran into Amir at the theater, and I've already had two unsuccessful nights with other men. One explained he was on antidepressants, and the other said he'd always had problems with sex. I've started to think there's a curse on me.

It was touch and go when I met Kemal earlier tonight at a Turkish friend's birthday party. We locked eyes immediately, and I was excited when he came over to talk to me. He wasn't just the best-looking man in the room, he was exactly my type: tall, lean, athletically built, with jet-black hair and fine features. I told him I was leaving for Baghdad in just a few days, that I wanted to see if I liked it enough to go back for a longer stay, maybe work in reconstruction. I would begin to learn Arabic, read the Quran in the original.

"Fuck Allah," he replied. "Fuck the Quran. I hate the Quran. I lost my faith years ago, when I read Omar Khayyám on a mountaintop one night."

I must have looked surprised, because he softened his tone and asked, "Do you want another drink?"

Over many trips to Turkey and friendships with Dina and other Turks living in New York, I'd become familiar with the hostility to religion of nearly all upper-class Turks. Still, Kemal was unusally vehement, perhaps because he'd once believed. Lose one's faith from reading poetry? I remembered the closing lines of the one Khayyám poem I'd read—laboriously—in Farsi:

> *From my coming heaven's wheel had no benefit—*
> *My going won't increase its dignity;*
> *And from no one did my two ears hear*
> *On whose account was this coming and going.*

It was a wonderful poem in the original Farsi, but the stuff to shake one's faith? Here was a seriousness about the written word I could only envy as a writer. I could imagine a fundamentalist Christian turning against his upbringing and cursing Jesus, but I couldn't imagine it happening because he'd read an eleventh-century poet. In Anglo-Saxon culture, poetry has not had such power for hundreds of years. But I'm learning the centrality of poetry to Arab and Persian culture, and I assume that it also holds a high place in Turkish civilization.

I let the topic of Allah drop, sensing that the cursing was part of a flirtation. And to my delight, Kemal turns the conversation to sex. At home in Istanbul he has a girlfriend, and he's convinced she's cheating on him during his three-week vacation in New York.

"Listen, this year in Istanbul I slept with one Italian woman who was on her honeymoon and another, Turkish, who was married for only one month. What does that tell you?"

"That you're cute." What it really told me was that Kemal is preoccupied with female fidelity and sends out signals that attract women who are promiscuous, or want to be.

"And you—do you sleep around when you have a boyfriend?"

"It depends. Anyway, I don't have a boyfriend."

Kemal was brought up in Europe, and his elegant English, typical of the well-born Turks at this party, has only the faintest hint of an accent. But his questions aren't an American man's questions. His directness and lack of subtlety remind me of Amir, and I respond as directly, without the effort at mystery I would have made with an American or European man.

We soon come to the topic I dread, my age. Kemal wanted to know the year of the first of my five trips to Turkey, but it was in 1978 so I don't want to say. He turns out to be thirty-four, the same age as Amir. I tell myself that it would be perfectly understandable if Kemal walked away, but instead he asks if we can go somewhere for a drink. I suggest my house, a little nervous because we haven't so much as touched. But when we get there things move very quickly.

We're almost as good a fit as Amir and I, and by any standards except those, we spend a long time having sex. But as we find our way around each other's bodies—and his is perfect, all toned muscle and graceful limbs and skin uncoarsened by age—I realize that he's without the slightest flicker of warmth. There's no love to be made here. But I am happy in a way. He's skillful, cunning, and virile, and I know I'll sleep well later, for the first time in months.

After a while Kemal says, "I wonder if my girlfriend at home is doing this?" He moves very far away, as far as my queen-size mattress allows, and begins to speak.

"If you get too close the sex isn't exciting anymore. That's the problem with most marriages. Couples should have separate bedrooms, the way my parents and grandparents did. They shouldn't sleep together like lovers, holding each other. And you don't need to talk so much to your girlfriend. You talk to your friends. When you meet a woman you want to fuck, you don't talk to her. You see if you like touching her, you smell each other. Then you go to bed together."

As we had, a couple of hours after meeting. I sit up straight, all languor gone. I can remember Amir's smell almost as if he were here now. Perhaps Kemal is right, though he admits he's never been married. Some of the marriages I know that have worked best are those where husband and wife spend a lot of time apart. My own longest relationship might have owed its durability to the months Scott and I spent living in different cities.

I've grown to agree that Americans are too quick to make

friends of their lovers, or to think that what they need in a lover or a spouse is another friend. If I can satisfy my curiosity about a man by talking with him, I don't need to go to bed with him. The ones I want, now, are those whose hearts I learn through their bodies, those I get to know by making love.

I want to put feeling first, now that I am so old it doesn't look as if I'll get married. This fate used to surprise me. I've had many lovers, men and women, nearly every kind of sex you can have, three proposals in my twenties. But it gnaws at me these days that there is something I never learned, something I tried to blunder upon but never saw for what it was. Maybe it had to do with not talking so much. Maybe that was why I dated so many musicians in my thirties—was it seven or eight guitar players, plus a few drummers? They didn't communicate best with words.

What would it mean for a husband and wife to be too close? Wasn't this a sad idea? Could I live with someone who wasn't my favorite person to talk to? Or is Kemal right? Am I attracted to men who are less verbal because this distance is erotic?

Kemal continues, "I met my girlfriend when she was with her boyfriend, an American. I asked for her number and she gave it to me. Turkish women are interested in American men. They're tall, blond, and they have the same accent as the actors in the movies."

How funny, after years of envying British and Italian accents, to realize that we Americans are glamorous for others just as they are for us.

"Later she told me that she lost respect for him because he let her give me her number. If he had been a Turk, I would not have asked. And if I had asked, he would have stopped it, or started a fight, or said something, something humorous. What's worse, her former boyfriend is still my friend! American men are not men."

"I worked in Russia for four years. I love Eastern European women. If they like you they will fuck you, and if they don't, they won't. There's no bullshit."

There is no courtship, Kemal may mean. Maybe he doesn't get it about courtship, the Western ritual in which a man feigns submission in order, ultimately, to dominate. Asking a woman for her number in front of her boyfriend? Bold and direct, but also crude and charmless. The sort of man who would do that might also ask another woman for her number in front of his girlfriend. This is the behavior of someone for whom all of life is reduced to power relations—a premise I've grown to find immeasurably sad and also boring, as it played out in the last couple of months with Amir.

"Women shouldn't be too nice to their boyfriends. You should turn us down sometimes. We like that."

Genuinely not being interested in a man is a proven magic recipe for obtaining his interest, but I don't want to play the game. I'm tired of being told I should act like a bitch, never show my feelings, keep men in line. What's the prize for all that falsehood? What kind of marriage comes out of that? What kind of person does one become?

"Your country is completely crazy now, with all these rules about sexual harassment. In Turkey the society takes care of sexual harassment. If a man is harassing my woman friend, I will warn him, and if he continues, I will beat him up. If a man rapes a woman and he goes to prison, he will be killed there. If a man in a subway molests a woman, he will be beaten up."

Whether or not this society works as promised, there's something inspiring about Kemal's description. And though he sees these Turkish customs and American laws against sexual harassment as an either-or proposition, there's no reason they couldn't coexist; sexual harassment could be both illegal and regarded as shameful. Part of the problem in the United States is that sexual harrassment isn't seen as shameful. Hardly anything is, anymore.

And part of the problem lies in the fraying of family ties. In Afghanistan, a woman who thinks a man is treating her disrespectfully can reproach him with four simple words: "Have you no sisters?" In mainstream American society this challenge would produce only bewilderment. Many men have such hostile or ambivalent feelings toward their sisters that being reminded of them wouldn't improve their behavior.

"It's the major leagues in Turkey. It is so difficult to get a woman there to go to bed with you. You have to make her jealous. I only go to clubs where I know a lot of women, so I can dance with one and then another. Just as soon as one of them is getting hot for me, I excuse myself and dance with another one. If I didn't do this, they wouldn't be interested. That would be overkill in New York; people would think I was crazy.

But in Istanbul it is what you have to do. New York is easy. I could sleep with a different woman every night in New York. You're the third in three weeks."

I've also been seeking consolation in sex, so I'm not offended. Kemal is my fourth man since Amir, though I don't want to play his game and say so.

"If I weren't staying with friends I could have fucked three more—an Italian woman who didn't have a place of her own, and two eighteen-year-olds I talked into a threesome. I met them at a club. One was Greek and one was Ukrainian. But they didn't have somewhere to take me."

As he pulls on his jeans I notice that they're peculiar; at the ankle there's a horizontal seam and a flared part like nothing I've ever seen on men's pants. Then he draws on a pair of terry socks, as short as the white ones with pompoms I wore as a girl, but black.

I laugh. I can't resist telling Kemal, "You shouldn't wear those in the States. Only women wear socks like that here. And one doesn't wear socks at all with those loafers."

He grimaces but manages a laugh in return. "I can get into any club in the world in these jeans. They are from an Italian designer; I forget his name."

I feel ashamed of my remark, which comes from disappointment in the prosaic end of the evening. I know better. What I loved in Amir wasn't his facade of sophistication (which was no sophistication at all in terms of my culture) but the poignant rifts in his efforts to be cool: his ugly tan loafers and cheap cracked wallet, his not knowing a thing about European food and wine, his unabashed delight in making love, the way he holds nothing back, the way he let me see him cry. But Kemal isn't letting me see much of his feelings. If he'd been vulnerable for a moment, I would have found his little black terry socks endearing rather than silly. But he isn't, or he's too sad and too guarded for me to see it.

I walk him downstairs, and as usual, my cats are on the couch near the door. Kemal kisses me on both cheeks, not on the mouth. Again I'm reminded of Amir. And then he reaches down to kiss Kimba.

"I have one at home just like this one but with white paws. I miss her. I can't wait to see her the day after tomorrow. Well, see you around. It's almost Friday now, isn't it? I have to find a mosque." And he smiles sardonically as he walks out the door.

A couple of months later, I learn from mutual friends that Kemal is back together with his girlfriend. She broke up with him just before he came to New York. Then I understand why Kemal pretended they were still together; in his obsession with creating jealousy he would have thought that having a girl-friend enhanced his allure in my eyes. Or was it, more touch-ingly, a type of magical thinking I'd also caught myself in? Saying it's over makes it real. And someone who lost his faith because of a poem or two might have taken words seriously enough to fear to speak those. As it turned out, his gamble worked.

But what interests me most about Kemal is what he said about not talking. *You don't need to talk so much to your girlfriend* can sound harsh to ears raised on endless relationship talk, and offensive to minds on guard against men treating women any differently than they treat men. A decade or two ago I wouldn't have liked it. But now I see it in another light. There's a line from Rumi I'd copied one hundred times with a bamboo pen, practicing my Persian calligraphy under Shirin's guidance: *Be silent that the lord who gave you speech may talk.* If we explore ultimate things when we make love, we learn more about each other in our silence than in our speech. Like the Rumi line, Kemal's advice suggests that the deepest and finest parts of our nature may not be in our speaking but in our listening, not in our intellect but in our feeling.

I blink in the relentless sun. In earlier travels to the Mid-East it's been a point of honor with me that as a Semite I don't need sunglasses in the desert my ancestors came from, but I might reconsider. The temperature must be one hundred and it's only eight in the morning. New York's damp, cold spring had matched my mood, and Baghdad's searing heat is a shock. Together with the pollution from the untreated car exhaust, it makes the air a felt presence as I walk into the al-Hamra Hotel.

This is where Dina told me to stay, but they're fully booked. She and her boyfriend Paul and Jason and Robert have all gone home now, along with many of the embedded reporters, but a new crop of journalists is taking their places, and their coveted al-Hamra rooms. I got a room at a much more modest place around the corner for twenty dollars a night, a third of the al-Hamra's price. For five dollars a night I'll be able to use the al-Hamra pool, the center of a nightly social scene that Dina described as the hotel's main attraction. The long blue rectangle of the pool is immensely inviting after the overnight trip from Amman in a car without air-conditioning, but I want to get to work.

I've come to the al-Hamra to meet Othman, who was Dina's driver when she and Paul reported from Baghdad a couple of weeks ago. Othman is of average height, maybe five-ten, heavy-set, with a fleshy, kind face and thick black hair touched by gray. I guess he's thirty-five. He has the same body type as Amir, and I can already see that it's a common build here. Like a surprising number of Iraqi men, Othman wears a plaid long-sleeved shirt. Perhaps there was a sale on tartan, or this is an odd artifact of the long-ago British occupation.

Othman's English is better than I'd expected. It turns out that until a few months ago, he was a commander in the Iraqi Air Force. He's an Air Force Academy graduate, trained as an engineer. He is a Sunni, like most officers. (When I've been in Iraq longer, I'll realize that Othman, like Abu Bakr and Omar, are among the names that signal Sunni heritage; they're the names of the first caliphs, whom Shiites resent.) He might have been a Baathist, and he certainly had kept his head down in the Saddam period. But if Dina and Paul had hired him, his politics must be all right. Dina backed the exiles' efforts to unseat Saddam since the first Gulf War, long before it became a favorite right-wing cause.

The calm oasis of the pool area is a welcome contrast with the chunk of Iraq I saw driving from Amman last night. That section is mainly desert, but ugly. It reminded me of the stretches between Dubai and Fujairah in the United Arab Emirates: gravelly rather than sandy, dun colored, and featureless. At least the UAE has hills. This is perfectly flat. There are palm trees, but not enough to erase the sense of a landscape mucked up by the hand of man. The spent quality of the land reminded me of Uzbekistan, and it might have been a residue of years of dictatorship. There is the feeling that someone powerful decided which areas to pollute and blot, as opposed to individuals reaching the same result by trial and error. Smoke hangs heavy in the air in many places, either from brickworks near Karbala or from power plants in Baghdad. There are no filters, and this, plus the untreated exhaust from many cars, gives the Iraqi sky a metallic *Blade Runner* look on bad days.

Othman and I agree on a forty-dollar a day rate within Baghdad, seventy-five dollars for trips outside. His car is a Toyota in taxi yellow, spotless although nearly two years old. Even the original UAE export stickers are fresh. Othman gets in and waits for me to choose a seat.

In Kabul I sat in the back while Farid drove, both for reasons of Islamic modesty and because I didn't know enough Farsi to talk to him much, anyway. If I were a man, I would have been expected to sit next to him. One of the ways Afghanistan can seem like a classless society is that male passengers in cabs and dignitaries with chauffeurs will sit next to and chat with their drivers. I wasn't sure what the customs were in the Arab world, but if I'd wanted to play the modesty card, I could have done so. With Othman, an officer and an educated man, I feel churlish doing that. So I sit next to him.

My first task is to find Ahmed Chalabi. He's leaving soon for the United States for his daughter's Harvard graduation, Dina warned me when we had dinner in Amman, and I want to interview him before he goes.

Now, in May 2003, Chalabi is seen as the American favorite in Iraq, but when I first met him through Dina, he wasn't well-known. She brought him to my house one night in October 2001. Besides Dina and her boyfriend, I had only two other guests, including an American expert on Afghanistan. I didn't know what to make of the balding, fiftysomething man Dina introduced simply as Ahmed from Iraq. Was he an academic, as his brilliant eyes, muddy-colored jacket, and comfortable paunch suggested? But his clothes were expensive, and he was unusually alert and tense. When he declined offers of wine, beer, and hard liquor, I finally had the presence of mind to offer an espresso, and he accepted. He was as smart as anyone I'd ever met, he had a mysterious allure, and though I didn't find him physically attractive, I felt it was an honor to be making coffee for him.

We talked about the Afghan bombing campaign then under way. I argued that the Taliban would fold immediately, while he was less optimistic. Ahmed complimented my Afghan expert friend on his recent testimony to Congress, and I wondered what kind of job he had that he watched C-SPAN all day. This was just weeks after 9/11, and conversation turned to the war against terrorism and American strategy in the Muslim world. Ahmed warned that the United States might lose the opportunity to prove to Muslim democrats that they had U.S. backing. "We thought you supported us when we rose against Saddam, and look how many of us died."

After an hour or so, I asked Ahmed who he was. "This is Dr. Ahmed Chalabi," Dina offered, "the head of the Iraqi National Congress."

"I thought you might be a professor," I joked, and he replied that he did have a doctorate in mathematics. I'd heard of Chalabi, but barely, and didn't want to reveal my ignorance. At the time he was just another of the cultivated, persuasive exiles spawned by tyrannies the world over. And I was much more interested in Afghanistan, where change was imminent, than in Iraq, which seemed stagnant.

The next fall he was famous—one of the mainsprings in the drive to war. Dina invited me to join her and Chalabi for lunch one afternoon. She said he had liked me and was impressed by my accurate prediction that the American war in Afghanistan would be short. I was flattered, and even more so when I realized how learned Chalabi was. Over lunch we discussed Persian poetry, and it turned out that he knew it well. He spoke eloquently about Arab culture and the failure of Arab thought: *After a while we were only interested in poetry and genealogy. Our best grammarians were Persian, and our best calligraphers were Turkish.* I sensed his disappointment in his ancient culture's decline. And then he spoke of what was looking more and more like an imminent invasion of Iraq. He cautioned that Iraq's oil revenue wasn't enough to pay back its massive foreign debt quickly; this was not going to be a profitable war for America. But I agreed with Dina that it was a morally justified one.

Othman and I set out for the headquarters of the Iraqi National Congress—the INC—in the country-clubby al-Mansur district. (Al-Mansur means "the victorious" in Arabic; Baghdad was founded by Caliph al-Mansur in 762.) The traffic is terrible, even with so many cars off the road because of gasoline shortages and insecurity. It doesn't help that the traffic lights are out because the electricity isn't working. I look up at the streetlights and wonder how safe Baghdad will be once the sun sets. Othman tells me that there's a 9:00 P.M. curfew for just this reason.

Baghdad is not a beautiful city. It could have been; it's perched above the Tigris, and there's an old section full of impossibly ancient houses, but they're in the last stages of disrepair. These thick-walled, high-ceilinged, airy buildings are cool inside even when the temperature exceeds a hundred degrees. If Baghdad were an Italian hill town, they would be renovated to within an inch of their lives, with cute window boxes of geraniums. But because rich people in the developing world want to live in garish modern villas uninhabitable except when air-conditioned, the noble old palaces are shabby and decrepit, and the poorest of the poor inhabit them. Al-Rashid Street, the former main shopping district, is lined with arcades and overhanging second-story balconies, but everything is crumbling. The great Abbasid and Seljuk mosques and medreses are run-down and unvisited; on two occasions I would be the only person at Medreseh Mustansiriyah, a huge, severe Abbasid masterpiece of the early thirteenth century, named after the caliph of the same name.

Chalabi is not at the Hunting Club, the guard at the entrance tells Othman, and I can't get a signal on my Thuraya satellite phone to call his deputy, Entifadh Qanbar, whom I also know from New York. I'm starting to wonder if I made the right decision in buying Dina's Thuraya in Amman for $650. The bulky dollar-per-minute phone only works here and there. The landline phones are still out of order in 70 percent of the city's neighborhoods. I am coming to realize that life in postwar

Baghdad isn't easy even for the privileged. Much of the time, you have to go to find the person you want to talk to.

Finally Othman pulls up in front of a garish mansion known as the Chinese House for the most spectacular of its architectural excesses. The building incorporates neoclassical elements, a pyramid, a modernist penthouse block, and, most strikingly, a red Chinese roof. I later learned that it had belonged to the head of the Mukhabarat, Saddam's dreaded secret police. It would never occur to an American to set up the headquarters of a political party here, but the INC aren't American. By chance, just as I walk up the gravel path to the house, past the parched grass and a few white plastic lawn chairs, Ahmed Chalabi strides confidently toward me. Chalabi has a big smile, as he deserves to, and he's thirty pounds lighter. He no longer seems professorial.

When we shake hands, we nearly laugh. The change of scenery from our last meeting at an elegant New York restaurant is surreal. The only similarity is his Western business attire: a long-sleeved yellow cotton shirt and gray wool pants that look unbearably hot. His only concession to the less-than-elegant conditions of postwar Baghdad is Tod's boots instead of wing tip shoes.

Inside he tells me he can only speak with me for half an hour before going into a meeting. Determined to show that I'm a serious political writer, not merely a cultural critic, I take out my press credentials. He smiles and says, "Put that shit away."

I want to ask him about the influence of cousin marriage and clan loyalties on Iraqi politics. I became fascinated with cousin marriage because of my experience with Amir and with Nabila's family, and I've recently learned that it's in my background as well. Two of my mother's older first cousins on her father's side married other first cousins, and one of her mother's aunts married a first cousin. I've started to read anthropological works on the subject after a recent spate of articles made striking arguments for the influence of cousin marriage on Muslim societies.

I hand Chalabi a piece by Steve Sailer, which he skims at lightning speed:

> In Iraq, as in much of the region, nearly half of all married couples are first or second cousins to each other. A 1986 study of 4,500 married hospital patients and staff in Baghdad found that 46 percent were wed to a first or second cousin, while a smaller 1989 survey found 53 percent were "consanguineously" married. The most prominent example of an Iraqi first cousin marriage is that of Saddam Hussein and his first wife Sajida.
>
> By fostering intense family loyalties and strong nepotistic urges, inbreeding makes the development of civil society more difficult . . .
>
> The fractiousness and tribalism of Middle Eastern countries have frequently been remarked. In 1931, King Faisal of Iraq described his subjects as "devoid of any patriotic idea, . . . connected by no common tie, giving ear to evil; prone to anarchy, and perpetually ready to rise against any government whatever." The clannishness, corruption, and coups frequently observed in countries such as Iraq appear to be tied to the high rates of inbreeding.

Chalabi snorts and snaps, "The Jews have had cousin marriages galore, and it hasn't hurt them." I'm afraid I've offended
him, though he isn't married to a cousin. Saller argues that
Iraqis used endogamy to maintain tribal structures, but Chalabi claims that Iraqi society is far less tribal than Americans
think, especially in Baghdad. Many Baghdad Arabs, he says,
couldn't even tell you what tribe they were. I'm gathering that
Chalabi feels a little slighted by all this talk of tribalism. Un-
derstandably, he's anxious to prove to Westerners that Iraqis
are modern and ready for democracy. But I'm not convinced
that cousin marriage is irrelevent. When he leaves for a meeting, I continue on the cousin marriage tack with the tall,
gaunt Iraqi American academic Kanan Makiya, author of *Republic of Fear* and other books.

In quiet but assured tones he comes out with a mini-essay:
"Tribal ties assumed greater importance in Iraq under Saddam because he destroyed almost all the other institutions of
a modern democracy. Since the modern state has not worked
out, people have turned to more basic units of society, but
turning the argument around doesn't work. Universities are
filled with people trying to find structural explanations for
complex phenomena, but this tends to essentialize the argument. If you're interested in endogamy, you should look at a
book by a French anthropologist, Germaine Tillion's *The Republic of Cousins.*"

I immediately sense that Makiya is another of the smartest
people I've ever met, and that I should stop talking about
cousin marriage until I read the Tillion book as I do when
I return to the United States. The rest of the afternoon, I
chat with other members of the Iraqi National Congress and

sit at the fringes of a couple of meetings conducted in Arabic.

When the sun sets at last and the heat abates, I'm invited to dinner at Chalabi's house with his daughter Tamara, his nephew Feisal, and another American, a middle-aged academic named Ted. This house is far more modest than the Chinese House but only a shade less garish—all white marble and shiny surfaces.

"We are not responsible for the décor," Chalabi jokes. He removes not only his shoes but his socks when he enters, and I remove my sandals. The air is scarcely cooler now that the sun has set, and we talk briefly about how these new houses are unbearable when the air-conditioning doesn't work.

"Aren't you hot in those pants?" I blurt out. I'm proud of what I consider my desert blood—I'm not sickened by the hundred-degree temperatures the way some Americans are—but I'm hot even wearing the lightest of linen clothes.

"Not at all. I find the heat invigorating," Chalabi says proudly.

Dinner is served by a manservant. We have lamb kebab with different *meze*—baba ghanoush, tomatoes, tabbouleh. Ted asks for tuna, explaining that he keeps kosher. "It is interesting that kosher meat is considered halal," Ahmed says, "but halal meat is not considered kosher. As far as I can tell it's the same process of slaughtering; the only difference is the spell that the rabbi says."

Ted winces at the word *spell*, but it seems accurate. I did not know that kosher meat is considered halal, but it makes sense,

since Mohammed swiped many elements of Judaism for his
new religion. The two slaughter methods are similar. When
Humayon's family killed the sheep in Mazar, the careful spilling of the blood into a drain reminded me of what I was told
in Hebrew school of kosher slaughter. Of course the little
blessings recited in Judaism and Islam on such occasions are
continuous with the words primitive tribes used to placate
their deities in sacrifice. Chalabi, I think, shares my preoccu-
pation with comparing Jewish and Arab practices, with trying
to figure out the contours and meaning of this complicated
cultural cousinship.

The talk turns to Persian movies, and we speak a little Farsi,
until it is painfully obvious that the Chalabis' is far better than
mine. I mention that I want to start learning Arabic, and Feisal
says that I can take over with his tutor when he goes back to
his home in Paris for a few weeks. He's a native Arabic speaker,
but because he was raised in France, he hasn't learned all the
grammar.

Suddenly Feisal gasps. "It's almost nine—the curfew. I'll go
with the driver to take Ann and Ted back to their hotels."
I had forgotten, as it is my first day in town, but the curfew is
taken very seriously indeed by the American soldiers who en-
force it. An overnight jail stay is the mandatory punishment
for driving after nine. On the way back, I agree to start Arabic
lessons with Feisal's tutor the next afternoon.

The al-Hamra pool is the perfect end to my first day. It's wonderfully refreshing to plunge into the cool water and swim
laps, and it's also wonderfully refreshing mentally to be in a
place attuned to contemporary Western aesthetics, without

garish ornaments and glittery surfaces. I'd noticed this in Afghanistan, where I breathed a sigh of relief whenever I entered a well-organized Western organization's guesthouse compound to find a thriving garden, the absence of trash, and, most important, order.

As soon as I walk in, a German reporter I know from New York calls my name, and I sit down with his friends at one of the white plastic tables around the pool. It's not an intellectual bunch, especially compared with the INC people I've just left. When I ask about trading books, I'm offered John Grisham. But all I have to do is sit down to feel, thanks to the skewed gender ratio, the sexual power I had at twenty-five. Journalists send me drinks, invite me to sit with them, stare when I walk past their tables—thirtysomething American men, the same ones who at home have forgotten how to flirt.

At eleven, the management turns off the lights for the night, and the few bodies still in the pool acquire a mysterious allure they may not have had when fully visible. I'm still at my friend's table when a man pulls himself out of the pool right in front of us. He's tall and carries himself with the grace of a professional athlete, and then, in a contradiction that endears him to me, lights a cigarette with a negligent gesture. His name is Doug. I'm smitten; I love athletes and cocky self-destruction. I carefully pull off the shirt I'm wearing over my bikini. Being too heartsick to eat for two months has done good things for my body, and I want him to see. We talk only briefly. Doug is a news photographer, and he has to get up at five the next morning to go to Kirkuk for an assignment.

Much of my time in Iraq is spent sitting in traffic in Othman's car under a leaden sky. It's rather like life in L.A., down to the cloverleaves and massive traffic jams, except that there's no Mexican food and the radio offers verses from the Quran. It surprises me to learn that Othman reads the Quran every day, because he describes himself as not very religious. He's certainly untraditional. He not only married for love but he waited ten years to wed his wife, Madiha. Their families opposed the match on the grounds that she was five years older than he.

This made my ears prick up. I was familiar from Amir with the taboo on a man marrying an older woman in many Muslim societies, though Amir and Othman both also mentioned the example of Mohammed himself, whose first wife, Fatima, was not only fifteen years older but a widow, not a virgin.

It's because Othman has told me of his courtship of Madiha that I violate my main rule on dealing with translators and drivers. As in Afghanistan, here I try to avoid discussing my private life. The last thing I want is a verbal pass, and I don't want to bolster the common view of American women as "loose" by discussing behavior that's typical in my culture but not in this one. But I take a gamble and tell Othman that my last boyfriend was ten years younger than me and a religious Muslim. "It didn't end well," I add.

Othman asks only one question, but it tells me I was right to trust his sensibility: "Do you love each other?"

I look out the window at the endlessly same sand-colored buildings slipping slowly by. I don't want Othman to see the tears that come to my eyes. I miss Amir all the time when I'm not interviewing someone or studying Arabic or flirting at the pool; I miss him in dreams that wake me into tears.

"Yes, I think so, but I don't think there's any hope."

"If you love each other, there is no problem."

And then Othman asks me if it's true that if an American woman doesn't like her boyfriend anymore, she just leaves him and finds another one.

"Of course," I answer. "If he's unkind to her, or she wants to marry him and he won't, or . . ."

I stop because Othman seems shaken, whether by the evanescence of love in our society—more than one boyfriend in a lifetime!—or for reasons lost in the language barrier.

It turns out that Saddam encouraged the showing of movies that portrayed American women as loose, though Othman is canny enough to suspect the stereotypes. He asks whether most American women wear miniskirts and sounds disappointed to hear that they don't. I wonder what movies he's seen; they seem to have been in the martial arts and action genres, maybe straight-to-video B or C movies made for the Third World and bolstering all the bad stereotypes about Americans.

There's sexual curiousity, even flirtation, in Othman's end of the conversation, but also a deep respect for love, a way of taking desire much more seriously than Americans do. Ten years is a long time for a man to wait for the woman he loves, even if he had other casual attachments. It's longer than most American marriages last.

I'm very curious to meet the woman who inspired such devotion. A week into my stay, when I'm pretty sure that Othman's repeated offer to come for lunch with Madiha is sincere, I accept. Their house is between the outskirts of al-Sadr City, the Shia slum once called Saddam City, and a more prosperous upper-middle-class district; the area is called Palestine, for the long main street, Palestine Street. The house is small, scarcely wider than my own narrow West Village brownstone, and Othman and Madiha live only on the ground floor. Upstairs is another apartment they are hoping to rent to one of the foreigners coming for long stays, but now it's empty.

Their apartment is small but bright and very clean, just one sparsely furnished room with kitchen appliances against the wall and, down a short hall, a bathroom and bedroom. Their four-year-old son, Aziz, sleeps in a small bed in a niche in the hall. He's playing at a local pool now with his cousins.

This modest place is in sharp contrast to the large, ranch-style houses of Othman's brothers which I visited a few days ago, and to the spacious flat of my Arabic teacher. I naively thought those were representative middle-class Baghdad houses, because there were so many like them, but now I realize they must have been upper middle class. After all, Othman is a commander in the air force, and even in the U.S., military men don't make much. In the living room, a cheap prayer rug, a plastic clock, and a few family photos are the only decoration.

Madiha is about my height but has a good twenty pounds on me; she's wearing paisley-print walking shorts that are too tight and a short-sleeved blouse. She looks like a California housewife of the sixties except for her elaborate makeup, pancake foundation, and high eyebrows colored in some distance above her natural brow line. I can tell, as I study Madiha's face, that she was once beautiful, and would be once again if she lost the extra pounds.

"I am so glad you could come here," she begins. "Othman has told me a lot about you. And we love Dina and Paul very much, and they also said you would be coming. The food will be ready soon. But Othman said you would be interested to find out what I think about my country. I don't like Iraq. I want an American government here. Only the Shia want an Islamic government. That is not good for Iraq. No freedom for women. It is not developed thinking. I want to make Iraq like America—no difference between women, men."

But luckily for our dining pleasure, Madiha has not put American principles into play yet. She has prepared a feast—a casserole of lamb, stuffed grape leaves that are the best I've ever had, an eggplant dish, pilaf, chicken. It's delicious, a far cry from the bland restaurant food I've been eating every day. It's probably also taken the better part of a day to prepare, and too much of the forty dollars I pay Othman. I feel bad; I suspect that they rarely eat so well. After Afghanistan I am alert to the fact that food costs proportionately more in these sparsely inhabited countries than it does at home. My restaurant lunch is four dollars, a *shwarma* at al-Saa'a is one dollar, but one hundred dollars a month was a decent salary under Saddam. As a military man Othman probably made less.

When I tell Madiha how wonderful the food is, she says, " Othman never praises my cooking. He says his mother's is better."

"My mother is a difficult competition. She is famous in our family for her cooking."

"It's hard for me to believe she is better," I say. "But anyway, Madiha is an amazing cook, and this is the best Middle Eastern food I've ever had." Madiha beams with pleasure.

Now I wonder about their marriage. Is the bickering over cooking a beloved ritual, or is Madiha hurt? Has she always been overweight? Or did she gain the extra pounds because of frustration or anger at Othman?

As I go about my business the rest of the day, first interviewing students at Baghdad University and then shopkeepers in
al-Sadr City, thoughts of Amir return. Amir is a physical absence as well as a heaviness in my heart that never quite disap-
pears. I remember his body so clearly, from the arc of his brows
to the too-hairy place just below his neck to his surprisingly
beautiful feet. Sometimes I hate him, but there are moments
every day when I need to cry.

The remedy for missing Amir might be an affair with an Iraqi,
if the right man materializes. The Iraqi men I've met so far have
a warmth and sweetness that reminds me of Afghans, joined
with a Western education. It could be the perfect combination.
And the Iraqis are "texturally correct" for me, as Rebecca would
say. Waiting in the long line of cars at the Jordanian border, I
watched perhaps the most attractive man I'd ever seen walk
past our GMC—an Iraqi, by his coloring and features. I never
ran into him again, but I realized that my penchant for men
who look like family but aren't could be fulfilled here.

But not at the al-Hamra, where I spend many of my evenings.
Occasionally I see an Iraqi, but he invariably turns out to be
someone's translator. The admission charge of five dollars a
day is too steep for most Iraqis, though on Fridays, well-off
families bring their children to the pool. Many journalists
have no Iraqi friends, though they might become close to their
translators. The language barrier isn't the problem, as many
Baghdadis speak passable English. And culturally, Iraqis aren't
so remote from Westerners; upper-class men often have university degrees from America or Britain.

Part of the explanation is the 9:00 P.M. curfew, which makes socializing after work hours difficult. Most foreigners stay close to their hotels at night, and the situation is worse for Iraqis, who are in greater danger if they violate the curfew. And I can't blame the journalists for wanting to be in an attractive little Western enclave after the dust and traffic of their work-day. Many of them have been here since the start of the war, and they're tired of hardship and hustle. Another part of it, I suspect, is American insularity; just because these people write for newspapers doesn't make them socially any more so-phisticated than their middle-American counterparts who va-cation in Provence or Tuscany without ever meeting the locals. And part is something worse, something about the Western attitude toward Arabs.

I catch a glimpse of these feelings, usually concealed by Amer-ican political correctness, when I raise the topic of sex. The journalists around the pool look at me as if I were insane when I ask if they've dated Iraqis, when I say that I wouldn't mind, that I think they're pretty cute. Then the prejudices come spilling out, a tribute to one of the last acceptable bigotries in American life: *fat Arab men, sexist Arab men,* and so on. A Euro-pean journalist, amused, points out that their insults could also be seen as fitting American men; it's pure projection.

I can't help thinking that the disgust these journalists express at the thought of making love with an Arab shows that they don't consider Iraqis fully human. And I'm hurt, too. Many Iraqis look like my own people. They look like Jews. If Arabs are fat and sexist to these Americans, what are they saying about Jews behind my back? Slurs against Arabs are, literally, anti-Semitism.

23 | *a bottle of good scotch*

The restaurant is the prettiest I've been to in my ten days in Baghdad and the only one with an outdoor seating area. The evenings bring a welcome fresh breeze to the dusty streets, and but for the hovering curfew, which forces us to dine at seven, we could be in any number of peaceful developing countries where the same tacky concrete architecture is in style.

As Doug asks me where I want to sit, I realize that I haven't been on a proper date in months. I haven't missed it, either; the format has long felt stilted to me. I prefer to get to know men more naturally, to invite a man to a dinner at my house, as I did with Amir, or to wait to see him over a period of time in a group of friends. People reveal themselves more quickly that way—or so I thought until Amir fooled me. But here in Iraq that won't work. Last night, I ran into Doug again at the pool and we talked long enough for me to see that the attraction was mutual. When the pool lights were turned off, he invited me to his room. He seemed kind and reasonable, a fairly mature thirty-seven, but I put him off. I suggested this dinner for no reason other than playing the American game. He has to pretend to court me. Even for a short affair, it won't do to be too accessible. Much as I'd prefer to be more spontaneous, I know that it works better this way with Americans.

Doug has lived in Italy for almost eight years, but he's too American or maybe too WASPY for me. Nothing says "family" about him—neither his cool blond looks and freckles nor his dry sense of humor nor his white-bread tastes in food. As I expected, he orders the least interesting items on the menu, french fries and kebabs.

As we're served our food, a bulky, good-looking Iraqi man in flashy clothes and jewelry comes over and hugs Doug.

"This is Yusuf. His brother-in-law was my translator a month ago, before he moved on to bigger things."

"Yes, now we are doing a lot of business together. Two restaurants, an Internet café will open shortly nearby, many projects. There are so many opportunities here."

I can't tell whether Yusuf is an MBA type or a gangster type, or maybe a bit of both. Doug asks if he still has Johnnie Walker Black.

"For you, yes," Yusuf says.

Although I've noticed already that he drinks steadily, Doug seems much more in control of himself than Amir, and his manners are much better. I wonder if we'll end up in bed tonight. I'm not feeling up to great efforts of seduction in my baggy linen pants and loose button-down long-sleeved shirt, sleeves all the way down in the ninety-degree heat for modesty in public.

I'm picking at the lamb kebab, already full on the *meze* I ordered, when Yusuf asks if he can join us. I would rather be alone with Doug, but Doug welcomes him. Yusuf sits catty-cornered to us both, and we talk about business opportunities in postwar Baghdad. Every now and then, to emphasize a point, Yusuf taps me on the shoulder and his eyes linger on me. I freeze. I have enough Iraqi friends to know that in this culture men do not casually touch unrelated women in public, period. My friends at the Iraqi National Congress and the other Iraqi acquaintances I've made shake hands with me on greeting and good-bye, and that's it.

If I were having dinner with Amir, Yusuf would never have dared to ask to sit at our table, much less to touch me. But Doug, a perfectly fine specimen of American manhood—with all the credentials from Division One tennis to three months embedded with our army in Iraq—doesn't register as masculine enough for Yusuf to respect him. And this has something to do with what I find lacking in Doug, too.

Doug has absorbed the lessons he was supposed to learn at his progressive northern California day school and at U Penn—that women are not male possessions and men are not meant to protect them. But after my time with Amir, the gender-neutral egalitarianism Doug takes for granted now seems ugly to me. I don't want to be with a man who thinks he owns me or with one who won't let me take the risks I want to take. But I also don't want to be with a man who seems indifferent to how other men treat me or to the assumptions they make about me. I don't want to be with a man who treats me as a buddy.

I can't blame Doug for being part of my culture, nor for his mild feelings toward me. He's no more in love with me than I am with him—he doesn't want to possess me, and only me, till the end of time. If I told him I wanted to go home with another man, he'd try to be civilized about it, and why not? But I would like him ten times better if he were not so adept at being civilized, if he put up the show of possessiveness Kemal spoke of, if he gave off the energy Amir did. I have to remind myself that Kemal and Amir weren't models for male kindness and responsibility.

When Othman comes to pick us up at 8:30, I wonder if he can read the unease on my face. I feel bad about sitting in the back with Doug while Othman drives. I respect Othman much more than I do Doug, and feel closer to him. And I don't want him to know I plan on going to bed with Doug tonight. It's not just my discomfort with contributing to the impression that American women sleep around. It's that Othman knows I'm still in love with Amir. I want him to think I take love seriously, too—as seriously as he does—and part of me is starting to. But I don't take love seriously enough to turn down no-strings sex with a handsome younger man.

Doug asks if I want to come to his hotel, an even nicer place near the al-Hamra. I wince, for Othman has surely heard.

"Why don't we get a drink at the al-Hamra?" I say with exaggerated emphasis, for Othman usually leaves me there at the

end of the day. And when Othman says good night, I tell Doug
that I want to keep my private life private.

Doug's room is a wonderful change from mine. The air-
conditioning works, the furniture could come from a luxury
hotel in the West, there's a bottle of good scotch open on the
coffee table. And then I see that there's also a bottle of good
scotch open in the kitchenette, and another bottle of good
scotch on the night table.

I feel a wave of compassion for Doug. Why is he as sad as all
these bottles suggest? I hardly feel up to finding out or inves-
tigating why I'm with another man I think drinks too much.
The point is to overcome my sadness. And I do. Doug is beautiful naked, I love looking at his body, and he's skillful in bed
in the American ways. And unlike Kemal, he shows some
warmth and kindness that feels intended for me. It is nothing
like being with Amir, but it is good enough for now.

The next night is Doug's last night in Iraq before going back
to Kuwait and then to Rome, and he asked me to spend it with
him. This is an emotional time for him. Like many of my
friends who worked here during the war, Doug has been surprised to find that he isn't eager to leave. He's come to feel
close to the Iraqis—Doug has Iraqi friends—and is fascinated
by their society. I wish for Doug's sake that he were with someone who cared for him as much as I cared for Amir; he seems
lonely and fragile. We go to visit his friends Pamela and Andrew in their suite at the al-Hamra. Pamela and Andrew are
also American photographers, and most of the talk is about
work. Andrew was in Afghanistan during the American war

there, too, and he loves the people and country. Pamela is skeptical and raises the usual Western objections about women and *hijab* and horrible sexist men.

"It is quite odd there," Andrew agrees. "I spent a lot of time on a story about families in Macrorayon, and it turns out to be a hotbed of anal sex." Pamela looks blank. "You know—the unmarried girls keep their virginity only technically."

Macrorayon is an area of large, depressingly run-down Russian-built apartment blocks that represented the ne plus ultra of Kabul sophistication before the war, when the water and electricity worked and the lawns and playgrounds were maintained. Many of the Afghans I knew had relatives who lived there at one point or another, and I'd been to an Eid party in one of the apartments six months earlier. It was hard to imagine the shy, badly made-up college girls I'd seen getting buggered in their crowded flats.

"I think a lot of the girls keep their virginity more than technically," I put in. "I dated an Afghan in New York and from what he said—"

"You dated an Afghan? What was that like?" Pamela asks sharply.

"Wonderful and terrible."

"I bet I can guess how it was terrible," Pamela says, laughing. "Arab men must be awful in bed."

I'm furious. I've never slept with an Arab man, unless you counted Amir in for his seventh-century ancestor, but I very much like most of the Iraqis I've met here. What is it that makes Americans say things about Arabs they would never dare to say about the Irish or about blacks?

"Afghans aren't Arabs," I reply. And then, casting all caution aside, "and he and the other Muslim man I've been with were amazing in bed." I glance at Doug and add, "It was out of bed that we had problems." Doug lets it pass. I sense he's also fleeing from a failed romance; part of our implicit bargain is to let our pasts alone.

Later that night, I have a dream that wakes me before dawn:

> I'm on my way back to my house and I spot Amir at a pay phone at the corner. It's clear that he's calling me, and I tease him about just happening to be on my very short street. Then we're in my house and we start making out. But before we can take our clothes off, Amir tells me he has a girlfriend and can't go any further.

When Freud met with his first patients, he developed the theory that the physical symptoms of hysteria that drove them to see him were the conversion of unvoiced and sometimes culturally unvoiceable complaints. Could these young women but say what they needed to say, their symptoms would disappear. Dreams, too, represented a language of the unconscious and, if correctly deciphered, told of the dreamer's wish fulfillments. As Freud never forgot, the dream speaks the primitive desires of the body. His famous dictum *wo Es war, soll Ich werden* (where it was, so I shall be) suggests among many other things that the body—the deepest levels of the nervous system, the part Mailer spoke of remaking—gets there first. It knows before we know we know.

By now I've decided that I made a mistake about Amir's character, but my body wants him still—him, not Doug, not Kemal, not the other men I've been with this spring. And so I punish myself for dreaming about Amir by making the dream unbelievable: Amir is addicted to his cell phone. He'd never use a pay phone, so I undo the very wish I have him enact. As for the girlfriend in the dream, I've heard that he's not seeing anyone, so I can wake up from that dream and reality is better, just as in the exam dreams of people long out of school.

But none of this changes the fact that Amir's already left me. I turn toward Doug beside me, but he's fast asleep.

My first days in Baghdad, I was relieved to find that Iraqis were far easier to talk with than Afghans. Superficially, Iraqis seem like Westerners, or smarter: quick on the draw, articulate, and direct. I never have the Afghan feeling that I have gone back in time, nor do I have that sense of the morning of the world. I keep thinking that Iraqis are a lot like Jews, cousins as we are. And many educated Iraqis are eager to tell you how rational, secular, and sophisticated they are. Like Ahmed Chalabi and Kanan Makiya, they downplay the influence of tribalism and tradition on their society. But that is just one layer of the onion.

I've been trying to interview as many people as possible, speaking to twenty or thirty Iraqis a day, asking very direct questions about their living conditions pre- and postwar, about their thoughts on Saddam, about the politicians who hoped to lead the new government, about democracy. From women who sell tea in the market in al-Sadr City to privileged university students, what I hear is that everything is terrible: the electricity, the security, the returned exiles, the politicians, the

Shiites, the Sunnis. I'd note it all down and then move on to the next person, who would say nearly the same thing. But if I asked, "So when do you want the Americans to leave? Immediately?" the answer is always a shocked "No!" Are Iraqis just terrible whiners? Or am I missing something?

"Iraqis are a completely frustrated people, so if you ask them anything they will tell you it is bad. If you told an Iraqi you were giving him a Toyota Land Cruiser, he would ask how you thought he was going to afford the gas." Iraqi National Congress spokesman Entifadh Qanbar tries to explain the paradox to me. We met in New York through Dina, when Entifadh was an INC activist in Washington. Fortyish and stocky, with thick dark hair, he is quick, massively well-informed, and devoted to Iraq. He fled Iraq in 1990 after forty-seven days in jail under political charges. He's lived in the United States ever since.

"You have to let Iraqis get to know you and talk with them for a while, and then they will tell you what they are really thinking. You hear them talking about the Americans doing this wrong and that wrong and then, twenty minutes later, they'll tell you that they love Bush, they would die for Bush!"

I curse my blindness. Entifadh's example reminds me of a joke Samuel told: A Jewish grandmother gives her grandson a red shirt and a blue shirt for his birthday. The next Shabbat dinner, he shows up in the red shirt. "So what's the matter with the blue shirt?" she asks. The Iraqis could have been my people, just corrupted by a dictator. Like the Jews, the Iraqis look back on a rough history. Baghdad was conquered in 945, in 1055, in 1258 (when it was one of the biggest cities in the world, and the Mongols killed as many as eight hundred thousand of its inhabitants), in 1339, 1401, 1410, 1508, 1534, 1623, and 1638 and that's before the traumas of colonialism and Saddam.

It takes time to realize how deep the damage Saddam did to his people goes. I hear one understated but eloquent story about Saddam's society from a rich scion of a Kuwaiti and Saudi family of sheikhs and pearl traders, Omar al-Ibrahim. An English-educated businessman in his fifties whose family once owned an apartment on Fifth Avenue opposite the Metropolitan Museum, al-Ibrahim smokes three packs a day. He matter-of-factly discusses the oddities of doing business in Iraq under Saddam, where bank loans were nearly unavailable, and anything could be confiscated by the Baathists at any time. There was no insurance in Iraq after 1991, either. In an economy essentially controlled by one man, al-Ibrahim explains, "if he killed someone he didn't want to pay for it."

As my weeks in Iraq draw to a close, I think back to my initial interest in cousin marriage. I hadn't been totally off the mark. Entifadh initially denied that cousin marriage was particularly prevalent outside of the Iraqi countryside. Then he paused and admitted that two of his brothers were married to first cousins, "not because they were interested in marrying cousins, but because you know that person really well, you know their family, and you know that both sides of the family are pulling together to support the marriage." The Saddam period had fostered social conservativism. "Other institutions in Iraq worked against you. The tribal system was the only way to establish a family welfare system." My Arabic teacher, a *sayeed,* or direct descendant of Muhammad, tried to interest his daughter in his sister's son. He must have been pretty unappealing, for instead she was marrying an Iraqi living in Sweden whom she had met just twice.

After visiting a half dozen Iraqi homes of different class levels, I have a new theory about cousin marriage and its relation to *hijab*. It's the opposite of what Germaine Tillion and the conservative thinker and anthropologist Stanley Kurtz have argued, that men protect close female relatives from contact with other men because they are secluding their own future marriage partners. What I've seen in Iraq of the sharp difference between women's clothing inside and outside of the home makes me think they got it backward.

The same university student who conceals her shape in a long-sleeved tunic and long skirt in somber colors when she goes out changes to a tight, low-cut blouse and short skirt as soon as she comes home. Matrons like Madiha walk around the house wearing shorts. And the young men of the house see nothing like this in the outside world. They're naturally aroused by the visible charms of their female cousins. It's not that cousin marriage leads to *hijab*, it's that *hijab* leads to cousin marriage.

Of course this view doesn't account for the fact that in Afghanistan I'd seen a much smaller difference between *hijab* and what's worn at home. But then, in Afghanistan even the well-off people I was among wore the same outfit endlessly, and women just added a *chad'ri* or a coat when they went outside. Some women I saw shopping in the bazaar in Maimana wore only a *chad'ri* over a long dress in the winter; they didn't own winter coats because they rarely went out of the family compound.

The gap between what Iraqi women wear inside and outside the home is reminiscent of the gap between written and spoken Arabic. While learning the language, I discover that the sharp differences between formal and informal, or between official and street Farsi, are paralleled in Arabic. Iraqi Arabic is more like dialect, an intimate language not heard on television or used in newpapers, where you hear and read formal or standard Arabic.

I remember Amir's use of French to proposition me, his embarrassment in writing words associated with sex in Farsi, and his explanation that "one is a different person in different languages." Arabic speakers, like Farsi speakers, might experience this to a degree that people who are bilingual in French and English, or Italian and French, don't.

All cultures have an inside and an outside, and as an American I might overread the gap between them. In the United States we have nearly erased the public/private division, parading our dirty linen on television and dressing in casual clothes at work. But this gap is essential to traditional Islam. And I'm coming to see that it's the source of both the repression and hypocrisy condemned by Western critics, and the sweetness and warmth I found in Iraq, Afghanistan, and with Amir.

The inside/outside division is not just about the seclusion of women, endogamy, and the maintainence of tribal ties. The gap is there because it makes it possible for people to survive in the outside world while enjoying love and warmth within their families. It's visible in the structure of Islamic homes and towns—the dirty narrow alleys contrasting with the clean and lovingly tended inside gardens and courtyards. The tender inside world it makes possible is a powerfully appealing place, so enticing that millions of people choose it over Western ideas of ease and freedom, so enticing that I would consider living in Kabul or Mazar-i-Sherif.

Amir is a product of this world and has its strengths and weaknesses. I'd come to dread the Amir I saw outside my house as much as I adored the man I saw inside, and when I wished he could be all of one piece, I naturally envisioned an Amir who was all vulnerability and charm. Now I see that the two seemingly opposite poles of his personality make each other possible. The man I loved in bed was so open and poetic and tender in private, precisely because he was defensive, suspicious, and hard in the outside world. Like their cultures, people must be taken whole. An Iraqi proverb seems apropos: *The one who enters between the onion and its skin receives nothing except a bad odor.*

The trip back from Baghdad to Amman is supposed to take twelve hours, but we are five hours at the border alone. The customs officers are going through every single car in exhaustive detail; I've heard they're looking for looted goods from Iraq which are crossing the border in great volume, anyway. I curse the inefficiencies and corruption of the Arab world as I wait. My driver—not Othman but a regular on the Baghdad-Amman-Baghdad route—dozes in the front seat. But I'm less agitated than I might have been, because I'm engrossed in a book, Philip Roth's *The Human Stain*. Doug gave me his books when he left. The Roth is my favorite. Although the love affair it describes is like nothing in my experience, I'm in the mood to draw from Roth the message that love matters above all.

It might help that I'm finishing the last of my duty-free scotch as I sit in the poor shade of the taxi, but my heart melts for Amir. All of the rage and disapproval I've felt toward him seems beside the point, as it has in my dreams. There, I am never furious with him, and he doesn't appear in a bad light. Now my conscious is catching up. *Wo Es war, soll Ich werden.*

Where it was, so I shall be. What matters now is how I felt when we held one another.

For most of my life I've intellectualized love, deciding who was worthy or good for me rather than following my heart. I've been so worried about making a mistake, bestowing love where it was not deserved or reciprocated, that I've made every other error in the book. And when I look back on a quarter century of adult life, I remember so few moments of love even in my romances.

Sitting in the taxi under a sun that hardly moves as the hours pass, it occurs to me that it's not only Amir who has an inside and outside problem. If I have a consistency he lacks, if I'm more or less the same person in all of the languages I speak and in all of the places I go, it's not because I've gotten where I wanted Amir to go, bringing the warm and tender inside person outside. It's that the outside person is in control all the time, except when I lose my temper. Even in bed.

I nearly laughed at Amir for speaking of *making love* our first night. I found him repressed and unsophisticated for being unable to talk about sex detachedly, as I could. I've always thought of my detachment as part of my recognition of just how important sex is, like my insistence that I couldn't be with a man if the sex weren't good. Over the years, that came to seem a less and less popular position. Maybe it was the fading of the sixties dream of emotional and cultural liberation through sex, maybe it was something souring between men and women, but as I got older I was amazed at young women's lack of interest in sex.

For the girls I met, recent graduates of good colleges trying to establish themselves in New York, sex "without a commitment" was like driving without insurance, and even the right kind of safe, secure sex was way down on the list of urban pleasures. A boyfriend was a companion for brunch and long walks and shopping trips. When I told some of my women friends how many times Amir and I would make love in a long night, they were disbelieving but not envious. They'd say something like, *How do you have the time?*

The more people—almost always women—told me how sex was overrated, the more I argued that it was everything. But I'd forgotten that the reason it was everything was the emotions it called forth. Amir and I spent all that time in bed because of how we felt about each other—what he referred to when he said, *It's not me, it's us.* And the reason he was unable to talk about sex casually was the same reason he convinced me that *making love* was the right phrase.

Just after Amir disappeared from my life, I speculated to Shirin that I would have at least thought Amir would miss me in bed enough to get in touch. It was one thing to want to eventually marry an Afghan, and another to date an American now. He'd created a problem where there was none: While I fantasized about something more, I would have been happy just to make love with him every weekend until he left for Afghanistan, and let things die a natural death afterward.

"But Amir is an Afghan!" Shirin said. "He can't just separate love from sex like that. He can't see you just for sex. He's not like an American guy."

I hadn't realized then, but I know now, that the sex had meant so much to me because Amir's whole heart was in it. The inside Amir gave himself up to it and made me able to talk about *making love*. The man who could have had a calm and rational weekend affair with me wouldn't have moved me as Amir had. He wouldn't have changed my life. The love that had been too rare in my life wasn't calculated and reasonable, and it didn't come to those who insisted on rules.

I came to Iraq to escape my failed romance and my grief, to escape the whole topic of love, to concentrate on politics instead, but I've ended up seeing love as more important than I did before. The warmth of the Iraqis, the understanding Othman offered, fit in with Samuel's remark that people in the Third World are nicer because they have no rules. But it's also part and parcel of a still half-traditional Muslim culture that takes love more seriously than Americans do now. Othman's earnestness about love and his ten-year wait for Madiha remind me of those Victorian love letters I read. And it's another reason to believe that American men today are responding to cultural cues, not biology, when they avoid marriage.

Our culture makes it easier to devalue love by the language it uses. *Lover, romance, making love*—even these words have come to sound racy or treacly or archaic. We have boyfriends and girlfriends, sex, and *relationships*—a term used only for business matters until 1944, if the *Oxford English Dictionary* is to be trusted. The *OED* cites *Rolling Stone* on the still-new use of the word in 1977: "People don't fall in love anymore, they have relationships." The writer saw a distinction between love and relationships, and for all that he wrote for a youth culture

magazine, he was dismayed. He saw that there was something
fallen about the world that had "relationships," and he was
prescient.

Relationships are part of the intellectualization of love that
has crept unnoticed into our culture. Relationships take root
in the mind, love in the body. We choose relationships, but we
fall in love. There's not much to say about love. We daydream,
we walk on air, we weep, we clutch a palm to the heart, we stay
up all night in longing or in the fulfillment of desire, and what
we say is more cliché than substance: I can't live without you,
I've never felt like this before, I'd die for you, I want to spend
the rest of my life with you, you're everything to me, "till death
do us part." These words are gestures, really, toward what the
body says.

But there's a lot to say about relationships: examining, analyz-
ing, dissecting, criticizing, rehearsing, and plotting. That these
are businesslike words of Latin derivation is no surprise. A relationship between a man and a woman—often called a sexual
relationship just to make everything perfectly clear—is meant
to be a rational undertaking. The talk of relationships is at
one end of the same continuum as conversation about real
estate, or profit and loss, or who should be the next assistant
vice president of the bank.

Relationships are part of a turn our culture has taken away
from both feeling and the body. We like to say that love doesn't
mean desire and that sex needn't mean anything. Now our
fondness is here and our desire there; our kisses, we say, are
inspired by lust, but our words by love. It used to be otherwise.

Once a kiss meant love, swooning meant love, and love meant the need to touch and possess the beloved. Once, feeling and body were as one in love.

Emotional closeness doesn't always make for great sex, but a deep sexual rapport usually leads to emotional intimacy. That's why lack of sex can destroy a marriage. As a friend reflecting on the end of his twenty-year marriage put it, "The problem with a marriage where you stop having sex isn't just the physical frustration. It's that you lose the only time you're vulnerable to each other." For years, I resisted that vulnerability, especially outside of bed. If I were one of the people who didn't fall in love anymore, it was because I forgot what romantic love is. And I was reminded by a man who claimed that it was an illusion.

Rebecca and Samuel's social world in Bogotá is so centered around extended family that even the threesome invitation I receive involves two of her cousins. I decline, not drawn to either one, and no longer able to cheer myself up by casual sex. My threesome days might be over, although it's flattering to be propositioned by an attractive younger man. Leaving for Bogotá just days after returning from Iraq in mid-June has disoriented me enough to banish thoughts of Amir, but I know they are never far—only waiting for the right chance to return me to insomnia and tears.

It's suggestive enough that Rebecca and Samuel's life here feels like Afghanistan West, another branch of the republic of cousins. Parts of Colombia are a war zone, and the rich have armed watchmen and bulletproof SUVs—only here they are Jeeps, not Land Cruisers. Rebecca and Samuel, second cousins, live in a large villa between the compounds of his father and brother. (The families in the three compounds all think of themselves as having very different aesthetics, but to an outsider the similarities are more striking: a predilection for modern art and old silver and a sober, luxurious minimalism.) Samuel's mother, now dead, was the descendant of generations of cousin marriages and the first cousin of Rebecca's mother.

The main difference between Afghans and these Colombians, besides the comfort in which they live, is that the people I'm among are all Jews. Many are the grandchildren of immigrants from Turkey who helped industrialize Colombia in the first half of the twentieth century. This Jewish community is a tiny and shrinking minority in Colombia, just five thousand people who have not yet immigrated to Miami or other places where kidnappings are not a way of life. And despite the anxieties of such a life, the Jews I meet here seem more relaxed than those I'm used to at home.

Talking it over with Rebecca, I decide that the difference is that her Colombian community is Sephardic, so called from a Hebrew word for Spain, not Ashkenazic, like most North American Jews. Although *Sephardim* now refers to Jews from North Africa, Syria, Turkey, Yemen, and other Middle Eastern locales, many of their families lived in Spain at one point or another prior to 1492. There are minor differences in the format of the services and the liturgical music, but the biggest is linguistic. Ashkenazim (a Hebrew term denoting German origins) speak Yiddish, and Sephardim speak Ladino or Arabic. My family is Ashkenazic.

Sephardim are very different from Ashkenazim, mainly because they're from non-Western countries. They never went through the Enlightenment, and there's no counterpart in their practice to the Reform movement started by German Jews. They tend to be less interested in doctrine and theology than Ashkenazim, and more concerned with observance and piety—less cerebral and more emotional. Perhaps this is why Rebecca and Samuel can participate in Jewish life, observing the rituals of the faith that I am too ambivalent to enjoy—the holidays and bar mitzvahs—despite their being downtown New Yorkers in good standing. Samuel even helps to bury the dead of the Bogotá Jewish community, which is hard for me to reconcile with his fashionable black clothes and fluid salsa dancing; my only models for observant Jews are New York Ashkenazim, and they're staid uptown types. These Sephardim are almost as different as Christians.

I realize this one night when Rebecca's sixty-year-old father, Eli, dances on top of a table at a club, his thick gray ponytail spinning in the air. Granted, it's a club he's an investor in, but I can't imagine any man in my family doing such a thing—unfortunately. Like Eli, the Colombian Jews I meet are at ease in the world, sensual, affectionate, and outgoing. They're businessmen, not lawyers or doctors or academics. They party, dance, play sports passionately, and take an unambivalent pleasure in family life.

These families are traditional; women have their place, mainly as wives and mothers. It's for this reason, I'm beginning to suspect, that the men of the family are warm and courtly, with little of the defensiveness and hostility of American Jewish men. Rebecca has read a lot of French philosophy and feminist theory, and she often jokes about the patriarchal society she lives in, but I can't help pointing out that its solidity gives her and her women friends a security and confidence lacking in American women.

Jewish marriages here last a lot longer, too. Rebecca married at nineteen, had her children while she went to college, and recently went back to school for a degree in museum studies. Although it is the opposite of the path most of my women friends have taken, it's followed by many women here. (Of course, it was made possible by family money. Most of us Americans weren't able to support ourselves, much less kids, in college.)

These Colombian Sephardim are the first group of Jews I've actually liked *en masse,* much as it shames me to admit it. When I went to Israel in 1999 I expected to feel like this, but instead, I came away amazed at how an entire society could be so lacking in manners. Colombia delivers what I was promised Israel would: an enjoyable model for Jewish family life.

Maybe I could be happy marrying a cousin of Rebecca or Samuel's but there isn't anyone single who's around my age. In Colombia today, as in Victorian America, men as well as women marry early and stay that way. Rebecca's two sexy younger brothers, still in their twenties, are looking for wives. Both of them are intent on marrying Jews, though they date gentiles. They have hardened their hearts against marrying gentiles, much as Amir has hardened his against marrying a non-Afghan.

My mood darkens with the talk of Jewish marriages, and it

darkens again when we all go to a Catholic wedding. The night
after the wedding I have a vivid dream.

> *I'm outside a church and my wedding is taking place, or about to,
> except that there are interminable delays. There are strange proces-
> sions and ceremonies that strike me as vulgar and circuslike. When
> will I make my entrance? Finally I go inside to find out what is
> going on. I scan the packed aisles and Amir isn't there. Then I ac-
> cost one of the priests and complain about the delay. "You can go
> around by the back door," the priest says.*

Amir might have been absent because he wasn't the man I
wanted to marry or because he was; the groom doesn't sit inside the church with the guests. But it was my dream: I could
have had him waiting at the altar or arriving in a car. I could
have been agitated about his nonarrival. I wasn't. That was
not the issue for me in the dream.

I know I can rely on Rebecca for a good Lacanian interpretation. And no sooner do I finish retelling it than Rebecca says,
"The dream tells you that your obsession with the Islamic
world is a back door approach to your Jewish background."

But isn't that a little cumbersome? Why didn't my unconscious save itself all the Farsi and Arabic lessons? And I'm
not so convinced I'm trying to go back to Judaism. Rebecca's
unconscious may adore Judaism, but mine doesn't. I am not
convinced.

The last night of my stay is Rebecca's thirty-fifth birthday, and
I talk for a long while with Samuel's father, Isaac, by the pool.

A widower for two years, he tells me that he wanted to bring his girlfriend to the party but felt uncomfortable about it. She's not Jewish. How could he flaunt a gentile girlfriend after insisting that his children marry within the faith?

"But it's different," I object. "Wasn't the point of that to have Jewish children? You've already done that, and so have your children. Can't you follow your heart now?"

And I insist to Isaac that love is the only thing that matters.

27 | *fake arabic*

Later in July, as I walk up to the door of my cousin's house in Westchester, a sign in Arabic script leaps out at me. *Why do they have their name in Arabic on the door,* I wonder, stupefied. On the train up to Westchester I'd been doing my Arabic homework—I'd just started to study with an Iraqi tutor—but I wasn't so far gone as to think it would be normal to have one's name up on the door in Arabic in America. I look at the blue and white tiles again and see my mistake. The letters are Hebrew. The characters spelling out their surname on the tile plaque happen to be among those that are very similar in both scripts. I haven't looked at Hebrew since Yom Kippur services six months ago, I've mainly forgotten how to read it, and I saw the letters as Arabic instead.

I think of Rebecca's dream interpretation: *Your obsession with the Islamic world is a back door approach to Judaism.* Hebrew and Arabic are related languages despite their different alphabets, with some common vocabulary and grammar.

When my Arabic tutor Hassoun asked me if I ever studied

Hebrew, I was ashamed that I hardly remembered any of it. "Arabic would be easier if you knew Hebrew well," he observed. I'd tried. When I was twelve I went once a week to after-school Hebrew school to prepare for the Torah reading at my bat mitzvah. I hated the classes in form and content. Printed Hebrew left me cold, and the handwritten script, which was substantially different, was indecipherable on the rarely washed blackboard. The religious content didn't speak to me, and I disliked the bad-tempered rabbi so much that my parents let me quit months shy of my bat mitzvah. How could they blame me? Neither of them had done their Torah reading, either—or, for that matter, believed in God. Judaism was purely a cultural or ethnic identity for my family.

In my late thirties, out of guilt more than real curiosity, I gave Hebrew another chance. I learned to read it again in two semesters of adult classes, but unfortunately for my progress, I still didn't like the language. I enjoyed the content of the commentaries I was reading even less. I hoped for ethical inspiration or pithy aphorisms, but I was unable to see the text I finally picked to learn, *Pirke Avot* (the sayings of the fathers), as more than narrow-minded and dull. Another part of my problem with Hebrew was the letters themselves. The look of Hebrew always seemed tacky to me, and I didn't like the typefaces in the Torah any more than I liked what was on the door. But now I see how similar Hebrew is to Arabic, which I've always thought beautiful.

Later that night, hearing my mother use Yiddish words while reminiscing with her cousins, I remember that my mother's first language, Yiddish, which uses a lot of vocabulary from German, is written in Hebrew. She told me she didn't read

Yiddish well, but I had to wonder if my dislike for the look of Hebrew had something to do with the place Yiddish held in my family. My mom spoke Yiddish to my father when she didn't want us children to understand, and my dad, who knew only a little Yiddish, answered in the German he'd learned as a student of engineering and chemistry long ago.

It might seem predictable that my brother and I would want to learn Yiddish or German, to penetrate this secret language of the grown-ups. And my brother's German is quite good. He's visited Germany many times and has a lot of German friends. But I went through a German grammar in grad school without absorbing much and failed to pick up the language in an adult-ed class when I moved to New York.

German and Hebrew are connected through their roles in Yiddish, and not in any other way I can imagine. It looks as though I didn't want to understand the secret talk of my parents, much less learn to speak it or read it. Perhaps in a reversal of Amir's formula, I feared that I would become a different person if I knew these different languages. The Yiddish-speaking person was apparently one I didn't want to be. It could be that the example of my parents' unhappiness was too depressing for me to take the risk. And so the back door—first Farsi, then Arabic.

That summer of 2003, Arabic was my only consolation. After I came back from Colombia, I tried to reconcile with Amir. First, I e-mailed him an invitation to my birthday party in late June, under the heading "peace offering." He didn't show up or respond; Don, who did come by, said that Friday nights were bad for Amir. The excuse was transparent, but since he could have said that Amir was still angry at me, I took it as mildly positive. Then a week or so later, Shirin offered to speak to Amir about me. She hadn't seen him since the last night I spent with him, when she thought he was being rude to her.

"What happened with you two isn't right. You have so much in common. When Amir and I were sort of seeing each other, he used to talk so much about you; he thought you were amazing. He had a crush on you. I'll talk to him. I think I can make this right." I gave her a wooden spoon to give him, a primitive utensil I bought in Colombia that reminded me of how he described the *aash* spoons of poor Afghan villages. But when she came over to see me after her drinks with Amir, she was upset almost to the point of tears.

"He took the spoon, but he won't see you. I tried to get him to come over here tonight with me, and he wouldn't. He doesn't want to be your friend. He says that you wrote him a nasty e-mail. I told him he provoked it by the way he treated you, but he wouldn't admit he did anything wrong."

"I wrote a nasty e-mail? You should have seen his reply. He said he didn't owe me any explanation for his disappearance because we had a "three-night affair." I mean, we were friends for a couple of months, we spent five nights together, staying up the whole night and most of the next day making love, and then there were two afternoons he came over. We had more sex in six weeks than most couples do in a year, and he—"

"You should forget about him," Shirin cut me off gently.

"Is he dating someone else?"

"He says that he's not seeing anyone, and he's going to wait until the right woman comes along, one that he might not feel so much passion for at the beginning, but one where love can develop. He's got problems with women, Ann, I've told you before. He's not worth getting upset about."

So while I'd forgiven him, he'd gone on hating me. This was even worse than the fight at the movie theater. At least then I was sure I didn't want him. Now I wanted him back and he refused.

I buried myself in Arabic grammar. Dense with rules, it leaves nothing unanalyzed and little to improvisation. While Yiddish seemed to make me anxious, Arabic calmed me. I also began to memorize a few suras of the Quran. Soon I understood why Amir and Othman read it often. I didn't find the content any more edifying than that of *Pirke Avot,* but there was something comforting in the repetitions, and the grace and euphony of the near rhymes were accessible even to a beginner in the language. Some of the suras were surprisingly easy to memorize. The opening verses, the *Bism'allah,* or *In the name of God,* often the only prayer a non-Arabic-speaking Muslim is able to read, fell trippingly from my barely trained tongue. I even found it easy to write from memory. And I quickly saw for myself that the big Sumatran batik hanging in my dining room did not contain the first lines of the Quran after all.

When we were still just friends, Amir told me that my brother was wrong. The white script, faded by time to the color of dust, was just squiggles. It was fake Arabic, a genre I was familiar with from early Islamic pottery. In a largely illiterate society, knowing how to write is a status symbol. Illiterate potters painted squiggles that looked like phrases from the Quran on their bowls and plates, fooling an equally illiterate clientele—making magic, but fake magic.

I had a fragment of such a piece myself, the bottom bit of a medieval bowl given me by Kamran in Mazar. It's beautiful: The blood-black script blazes with the sureness of early Islamic art against the thick Mongol-era pottery. When he gave it to me, Kamran told me the script was the name of the Prophet, but again Amir said no, there was an *m* and even an *h* but the rest meant nothing at all. For a few months I kept it on the table next to my bed, but Amir kept using it as an ashtray, whether because it did not have the name of the Prophet or because it tried to—I could not tell. I was afraid Amir would ruin its white with ash, so I moved it to another room.

By the time I memorized the first sura of the Quran, I started disliking the batik. Like the pottery shard, it even struck me as irreligious. Though I was a nonbeliever, I saw a sense in which faking the name of the Prophet was blasphemous—similar to making graven images, which both Islam and Judaism fear. Or maybe the meaning of fake Arabic was more complicated. I thought of the ancient Jewish tradition where the name of God is not written out in full but (as it would be in English) as G–d, as though exposing it would diminish its power. Maybe some, if not all, fake Arabic was deliberately so, shielding the holiness of the name of the Prophet and the words of the Quran.

One day in September, when we were working on a Farsi lesson at the table underneath the batik, I told Shirin how I felt about it, and she said, "The person who made it was trying to make something beautiful, and he succeeded. In his mind the squiggles meant something, and who knows, maybe it isn't even from the Quran. We don't know what he had in mind because he couldn't write it! But you shouldn't look at it as fake Arabic. It's real art."

Then I saw a possible pathos in the batik. If it was not deliberate, it was sad. That artist would never read the Quran, or anything else. He was cut off from a pleasure that for me and many others was one of the main joys of life, an act I could not imagine living without. And he not only knew that the word of God was to be glorified in art, but also that he was only mimicking a pleasure he would never fully taste. There was something quintessentially human about his making a thing of beauty out of his longing and ignorance.

I also saw a pathos in my literalism, even in my passion for other languages, for Arabic. Wasn't there something sad about believing that my understanding of the world and of other people would be increased by learning so many tongues, when I had failed to find one man who could, in the American phrase, "speak my language"? Perhaps most lives offered no more; in most ways I'd led a favored time on earth. At least I had the chance to try for the understanding that eluded me. And if others had found this so easy, would we have the hundreds of languages and dozens of literatures our ancestors have left us? What would have been the need for language if our bodies told all, or if we could read them right? It is not just that tears come where language breaks: Language comes where tears are not enough.

In the unbridgeable space between people stands language and everything we make of it. To study many tongues is to explore many different monuments to isolation, misunderstanding, and sadness. Fake Arabic and every other form of art mark this terrible gap between hearts. Into this void we have willed God. The Quran begins, *Bism'allah* for good reason, just as the Torah starts, *In the beginning was the word.*

It's just before Christmas, a year after I first admitted to myself that I was falling for Amir and six months after my nasty e-mail to him. And I'm writing Amir a letter, a real letter, on paper.

Would it surprise you to know how much I cried after you disappeared from my life? It surprised me—I've never been the crying type. I should have learned how to cry much earlier, but better late than never.

Amir jan, I'm sorry I tried so hard to hurt you, and not hard at all to tell you how very fond I was of you. Your openness made me fear for you and want to protect you, but I didn't do that. I never opened my heart to you; I didn't have the guts. Maybe you understood me anyway. I very much hope that you saw in my eyes more than I had words for.

This is the first love letter I've written since college days, when Scott was at Oxford for a year and we stayed in touch mainly by the post, as everyone did then. I've written e-mails telling

men that I loved them, but not letters. Not in years. Not to
Amir, either, after our first fight, when he thought I might
have, and when, perhaps, I should have. That fight seemed so
sweet now in retrospect, and I was full of hope when we made
up. Eleven months later, I have almost none.

This letter wasn't even my idea. It was Shirin's. She hasn't seen
Amir in six months because she disapproves so strongly of
how he disappeared on me and refused to talk with me. When
he e-mails now and then, suggesting that they get together,
she makes an excuse. But when I talked with her a few weeks
ago about calling Amir, she advised that I write to him instead.

"If you call him he probably won't pick up the phone. A letter
would be good. There's that distance. He can come back to it,
he can think about it. He is a spiritual man, he has a higher
side. There is a lot that is bad about Amir, but there is also a
lot of good in him. Maybe if you appeal to his higher side, at
least he won't be angry at you any more. He may not want to
see you—he still has a lot of problems, he wants to marry his
cousin, he's afraid—but it might do some good. But I don't
know how much he's going to change. He's a grown man."

I'm as dubious about Amir's ability to change as Shirin is. And
even if he could show a new capacity for forgiving and asking
forgiveness, I'm not optimistic that anything would come out
of it. The reason is that words don't mean the same thing to
me and Amir.

Looking back, I've come to think that Amir's words are often
gestures, and nearly weightless. He says that he'll marry a

cousin, or that he'll go to Afghanistan, or that I'll have plenty of time to show him my bad temper when he gets back from Afghanistan, but all he means is that, at this moment, it sounds like a nice idea or it will produce an effect he likes in the person he's talking with. It doesn't express an intention. There's not necessarily any link with action. He hasn't married his cousin or gone to Afghanistan yet (so I know from Shirin). And he certainly isn't putting himself in the way of my temper, bad or not. Words and feelings can coincide for him, sometimes in moments of grace I can't match: *Hope must be created.* But the link is aesthetic, not moral, and it doesn't last.

Being held to something he said at a particular moment, or even frequently, might seem as bizarre and distasteful to Amir as having the same thing for lunch every day for a year. And that makes me guess that the dramatic reconciliation I've fantasized about will never happen. As Shirin told me in the summer, he doesn't think he did anything wrong. And my last e-mail might register with him more as a slap in the face than the moral judgment it was. The reason I'm writing this letter, though, is that it was a judgment on me, too. I chose to attack, and that said something about me. I was too scared to ever tell him in words how much I cared for him. Amir had not been brave, but it was the fear in myself that I hated in him.

I look at my handwriting on the cream-colored stationery as I copy from the computer screen. I started the letter in a notebook, but after a few sentences I switched to my laptop. I can't for the life of me compose on paper anymore. Amir wasn't impressed by my Farsi calligraphy when I showed it to him with misplaced pride a year ago; he will soon see that I have bad handwriting in English, too. But now I know what I didn't know then, that admiration and love are not the same thing.

When I was not yet nineteen, I went to a summer party given by a college acquaintance and met Scott. I found myself talking about my feeling that every hour of my day was scheduled with some activity of self-improvement. There was no time to live, between studying ancient Greek and running six miles a day, playing squash and attending classes. Of course this was what I was supposed to be doing; I was a college student. And I was familiar enough with psychoanalytic ideas to know that I fit every cliché of the child who had internalized the standards of her exacting parents. I don't recall that Scott said much; he was at heart a listener. But twenty-six years later I remember that as I spoke, I half knew I was really talking about something else.

I was trying to talk about this performance of the self, of the adult I was just then beginning to craft. And—though I would never have admitted it at the time—I was trying to talk about love, and why and where we love. At that age, I was convinced that love was based upon an appreciation of good qualities. Intrigued by Scott, I was wondering what he thought of me. Was I pretty enough, cultivated enough, to hold his interest? He knew a tremendous amount about music and art and history. I was terrified that he would find I fell short. But my unconscious knew that it was really something else that would determine whether we became lovers, something that had nothing to do with my roster of achievements and skills.

As it turned out, Scott did understand the underlying meaning of my rambling speech. He did find me lovable, lovable enough to be his girlfriend for seven years, but probably for reasons very different from my schedule of activities. And when he no longer wanted to be with me, it wasn't because I had fallen off my squash game or got a bad haircut.

The possibility didn't occur to me when I was with Scott that it was simple affection that he looked for in me, before talent. And it hadn't occurred to me that I might have grown close to Amir not because he fought for his country and spoke really good English and was witty and quick and a good cook, not because he had beautiful hair and soulful eyes, and not even because we had an extraordinary physical rapport, but because when we first became friends, he was kind and genuine, and that had allowed me to be the same.

A tear falls on the page and I wipe it away, then smile. I wrote about tearstains ten years ago, wracking my brain to think of evidence of human feeling that paper reveals and e-mail does not, and I came up with tearstains. And here one is. I continue. *I haven't forgotten you, and I won't.*

That is true enough. I pause, unsure how to end.

Now I'm less inclined to see what happened between me and Amir in terms of good and bad behavior. We failed each other and failed ourselves. I could do nothing about his shortcomings; perhaps he couldn't, either. Perhaps things could not have happened any other way, but I could acknowledge my faults.

I was too afraid to care for him or to show him the warmth and acceptance I wanted to give. For reasons that had to do with my own family background, I was impassive when Amir confessed his deepest fears to me, offering him arguments rather than comfort. He showed me an unconditional acceptance that assuaged my fears, and I challenged his worth as a person. For someone who talks so much, I was unable to say the right words at the right time.

Just a few nights ago I had a dream that terrified me. It was the first dream about Amir I remembered in months, although I suspected that I dreamed about him every night.

We're lying together on the sofa where we spent so many hours making love, but I know it's after the bad things have happened between us, and I'm wondering if we will touch. We're moving closer to each other, looking into each other's eyes, and I feel great fondness for Amir. Just then, someone interrupts. It's as though we're in a hotel and room service comes in. Amir scrambles to get his clothes from the floor. And I realize to my horror that we're in my parents' bedroom in my childhood home.

The dream was crushingly literal, and on one level hopeless: I was alone because I couldn't get out of my parents' bedroom, not at the age of forty-five. But it also showed that I had not given up yet. There's a cliché that a marriage has to work in the bedroom, the kitchen, and the living room. Amir and I had everything two people could have in the bedroom, and we did as well as I ever did with anyone in the kitchen. But in my actual living room, we mainly made love, on that very couch. And in the metaphorical living room, when we were together in the social world, Amir mainly was unkind to me. My dream wanted to bring the inside and the outside together, bring the outside-room furniture that I associated with joy into the bedroom, where I doubted my parents knew any. The dream image evoked what I felt while cooking with Amir, that keeping house flows naturally out of making love.

All of a sudden, I fully understood my Bogotá dream of the church wedding. It wasn't just about Judaism and Islam. I waited outside, single, in the cold world unknown to pleasure, but I disdained what went on inside, in the family world, which was too vulgar—that is to say, emotional—for me. The family world of my childhood was frightening and negative: a loveless marriage, my father's illness, his family incest. The emotions were overwhelming but mainly disturbing, so I blocked them out. And now I wanted in, but the only way I found was through the back door. My love affair with the Islamic world was a back door approach not to Judaism but to family.

In the West, a family unites inside and outside, in the house and in the public. One of the ways it does this is by bringing together in marriage people who aren't related. It joins members of the public who have fallen in love or have decided for whatever reason to share their lives, in a private intimacy. And in the advanced democracies, this private sphere exists not only to nurture the next generation of the clan but to also provide an entrance to and training for public responsibilities and ambitions. Loving outside the tribe and family then becomes a natural stage leading to the joining of yet other unrelated people in relatedness.

This process misfired in the case of my family. We didn't know how to marry people who were not family, and we couldn't marry those who were. That is why I was comfortable in the republic of cousins and found Nabila and Abdul Hasib's compound in some ways more natural than the house of my childhood. That is why I was still struggling with moving my sofa to my parents' bedroom and myself to the inside of the church.

How can a life be made right? The passage from Norman Mailer I read to Amir our last weekend together, nine months ago, comes back to me: "For if he has the courage to meet the parallel situation at the moment when he is ready, then he has a chance to act as he has never acted before, and in satisfying the frustration—if he can succeed—he may then pass by symbolic substitute through the locks of incest."

I so wanted to get there with Amir; I tried as hard as I'd ever tried with anyone. It wasn't enough. Maybe nothing would have been. Maybe I had whatever courage I had because I knew the deck was stacked against me and losing was to be expected; maybe it was like the way I can play my best tennis with people like Samuel, who are vastly better. But even if I didn't take the risks I should have, I treated Amir well when we were together. And things ended worse than with any other man I'd dated. Amir was the only one who wouldn't talk to me.

I will not ask to see him. I will ask for nothing. "All demands are demands for love," Lacan wrote, and I do not want to ask for love. I've done too much of that in my life. When I was young it never occurred to me that treating a man well and making him happy could be a source of pleasure in itself. When I was with someone for a year or more, I enjoyed showing him that I cared for him, but only when I was completely sure my feelings were reciprocated, and then some. I enjoyed

being in love, but it was for the sensations it gave me, not for
how it made the man I cared about feel.

I think of something Luisa said to me recently when I remi-
nisced about Amir. "You know," I told her, "even if things had
gone well, even if we were still seeing each other, I wonder if
I'd be happy. It was all about Amir's problems and Amir's anxieties. I don't know that he would have been able to help me if
I were depressed or had a real problem. He didn't offer me very
much in some ways."

And Luisa, usually so cynical, looked grave and said something that silenced me: "Except for the gift of loving someone,
which is incalculable."

Chewing on my pen, I remember two men who told me they
loved me years ago—my drug buddy Dave and my much-older
boyfriend Ben. I failed to reply, *I love you, too,* even though it
was what I most wanted to say in the world. And when I mentioned it later to Ben when he broke up with me, he said, *I was
drunk.* It took me a year to get over that. When Amir slurred to
me, *That's why I love you so much* on our first night together, I
ignored it because I was afraid he would take it back if it were
acknowledged, and I didn't think I could stand that.

Amir might not deserve my love or my mourning or this letter. Then again, the men I treated callously over the years did
not deserve that either, and I did not deserve the love I received
but did not return. But I have stopped feeling that love is
about deserving. Over the years I spent much time worrying
that I might be treating a man better than he deserved—and
no time at all wondering what I was really so afraid of. When I

lie someday on my deathbed, will I be worrying that I was more tender with Amir than he was with me?

Hope must be created. They were beautiful words but perhaps not meant for either me or Amir. The love we made sprang from a lack of hope. There was something deeply troubling in Amir, as there was in me, and I no longer have any American optimism that either one of us will escape our histories. But I still believe in moral experiments, and this letter, however hopeless in practical terms, is one of those. Simply having been sent such a letter will change the recipient's view of other people and their possibilities; it will enlarge the world that he sees. It is probably the only such letter Amir has ever been sent or will be sent. And even if he truly has a heart of stone, even if he rips my letter into tiny bits and manages to forget it, I will be changed by the act of having sent it.

It's not that I'm doing it for myself. I'm doing it to become the person who would do it for someone else. That much is possible, and I want it. Not so many years ago, I ended an essay with the words of Adorno: "wrong life cannot be lived rightly." But after the political events of the last few years, they struck me as irresponsible and evasive. Injustice is not an excuse for throwing up your hands and giving up, either in public or in private. The more wrong life is, the more it must be lived rightly.

Where did Amir, or I, or so many people today get the idea that it is a sign of weakness or foolishness to tell another person of our love? Our ancestors were proud to declare themselves, even when they knew their love was hopeless. Why, in twenty-five years of adult life, have I never been the first to tell a man I loved him? What good will it do me in the grave to have held my tongue?

I can't forget how Amir made me feel when we were together— the sweetness of touching him, the love I felt when he held me, the complete acceptance he gave me. I hope he felt loved by me. And if he didn't, I hope he will when he gets my letter.

And so I finish.

And I will tell you now what I should have said at the right time. You have my love.

Moral experiment or not, I still can't write, *I love you.*

Before I can change my mind, I fold the notepaper and put it in an envelope. I write the address of the Brooklyn apartment I was never invited to visit, walk out the door and around the corner, and put the letter in the mail.

glossary of farsi and arabic words

Aash Farsi—a thick Uzbek Afghan soup; also a somewhat different Iranian soup.

Abaya Arabic—a black floor-length veil leaving the face uncovered, worn by women in Iraq; also refers to an element of traditional Iraqi male dress, a black overtunic available in either thick or filmy versions.

Aya Arabic—"excellence"; the term for a verse of the Quran.

Bism'allah Arabic—the first, seven-line sura of the Quran.

Chad'ri Dari—full veil fitted to the head, with small eye opening, traditionally worn by some women in Afghanistan; known in Arabic as "burqa."

Chador Dari—head scarf leaving the face uncovered. In Iran, the chador is similar to the Iraqi *abaya* and also leaves the face uncovered.

Dari Afghan dialect of Farsi (Persian); along with Pashtu, one of the two major languages of Afghanistan.

Eid	Arabic—a holiday; here, contextually, refers to Eid al-Fitr, the holiday marking the end of the fasting month of Ramazan.
Gosfand	Farsi—a sheep.
Hadith	Arabic—a verified saying of Mohammed. Sunni and Shia Muslims do not agree as to all of the authentic *hadith*s.
Halal	Arabic—meat from animals killed according to Islamic rules of humane slaughter.
Haram	Arabic—prohibited under Islamic law.
Hijab	Arabic—modest dress generally; specifically, a head covering.
Jan	Farsi (also Arabic)—dear, soul, life.
Khanum	Farsi—Mrs., Madam, lady; wife.
Lala	Farsi—older brother.
Norouz	Farsi—Persian New Year, approximately March 21, celebrated in Afghanistan, Iran, parts of Iraq, and parts of other Middle Eastern and Central Asian countries.
Ramazan	Arabic—lunar month of fasting ordained in the Quran.
Sayeed	Arabic—a descendant of Mohammed.
Sh'ma	Farsi—formal and plural form of "you."
Sh'rub	Farsi and Dari—an alcoholic drink; in Arabic, a beverage.
Shalwar kameez	Farsi—ensemble of baggy drawstring pantaloons, or *shalwar*, voluminous but narrow at the ankles, traditionally worn by men in Iran, Afghanistan, and the Indian subcontinent with a *kameez*, or long tunic.
Sura	Arabic—chapter, one of the 114 major sections of the Quran.

acknowledgments

My gifted Arabic teacher, Dr. Ameer Hassoun, has patiently shared his knowledge of the Arab world, the Quran, and the hadiths. Kanan Makiya's suggestion that I read Germaine Tillion's *The Republic of Cousins* shaped this book and my thinking, and I'm indebted to Rosanne Klass's insights into Afghanistan, both in conversation and in her writings. I will always be grateful for the kindness of Omar Sa'ed in Baghdad and for the generous friendship of Asla Aydintasbas, who introduced me to Omar and to Entifadh Qanbar and Ahmed Chalabi, who have shared their own deep insights into their country and Arab culture.

I owe a debt of gratitude to the many editors who worked with me on material about Afghanistan and Iraq, including Mark Cunningham of the *New York Post* op-ed page, who patiently initiated me into the fine art of the seven-hundred-word essay; the indefatigable and encouraging Kathryn Lopez of *National Review Online,* and Doug Cruikshank, Suzy Hansen, Priya Jain, and Andrew O'Hehir of *Salon.* A special kudos to Laura Miller at *Salon* for conscientiousness and rigor well beyond the call of duty. I am equally grateful to Maria Russo for her help with my "al-Hamra pool" piece for the *New York Observer,* which laid the groundwork for the similar material in chapters twenty-one and twenty-two. Much of chapter twenty appeared in somewhat different form in *Salon.* I also owe much to Charles Lindholm's writings on Afghanistan and to Lila Abu-Lughod's superb book *Veiled Sentiments* on Bedouin culture.

I was lucky to have the hospitality and encouragement of Skat Smith in Auckland while I wrote some of this book, and of Jean-Michel Doublet in New York and George Dawes Green in Savannah while I edited it. Tim Wilson was always there when I needed advice and, more importantly, friendship.

Don Fehr, who edited my first book at Basic Books, read an earlier draft of this one and gave me crucial structural advice. More importantly, he believed in the idea almost before I did. Tina Pohlman, who also edited my first book in paper-back, took an even greater leap of faith, and an extraordinary gamble with her time, which I hope is now partly repaid. Her good influence is on every page, and her friendship is an unexpected gift.

My mother, Bernice Nachman Marlowe, was diagnosed with inoperable cancer when I returned from Baghdad in July 2003 and died just after I turned in the manuscript of this book in December 2004.

Her intellectual integrity and curiosity helped form me as a writer and person, and her perseverance in the face of long odds gave me an example to live up to. She was the first person who believed in me as a writer, and anything I write is in her honor.

Most of all, my gratitude to the love, wisdom, and often-tried patience of Roberto, Emma, Jessica, Silvana, Raha, and the remarkably warm, open-minded, and gracious "Faryabi" family of Mazar-i-Sharif. My weeks in their house changed my life. This book is for all of these dear friends.

author's note

The names of all of the characters who are not political figures or my ancestors have been changed. In some cases identifying details such as nationality, place of residence, or appearance have been altered. "Ben," "Dave," and "Scott" also appear in much greater detail in my first book, *How to Stop Time: Heroin from A to Z* (Basic, 1999; Anchor paperback, 2000).

Amir's identifying characteristics have been disguised, sometimes considerably. I've kept to the dialogue and sequence of events as closely as memory permits.